M000230122

"The wakeup call I didn't realize I needed.
Tracy is a MUST HAVE in your mental toolbox."
—DANIELLE IGOE, ASSOCIATE VICE PRESIDENT, THE CARLYLE GROUP

"Written in a no-nonsense yet supportive way, the book
challenges readers to reconsider their actions and take
responsibility for changing their lives. A powerful reminder
that you are worthy, and you are enough."
—CARLY CHEESEMAN, EXECUTIVE EDITOR

"As a self-proclaimed recovering control freak and perfectionist,
this book is IDEAL. Tracy's no-bullshit approach to personal
choice, her humor, and spot-on insights feel magical."
—JEN GUFFEY, DIRECTOR OF TALENT ACQUISITION, PRUDENTIAL

"I used to be so scared to show up and take action because of
what people might think. Not anymore! This newfound confi-
dence is amazing. I feel unstoppable. Tracy is the real deal."
—BREANNA KULWIN, TEEN EMPOWERMENT
COACH AT BREANNA KULWIN

"Tracy Litt is a powerhouse. Her intuition, openness, depth
of knowledge, and overflowing heart come together in the
ideal formation of gentle guider and firm ass-kicker."
—RACHEL SLOTNICK, CEO AT MINDSTRONG FITNESS

WORTHY
HUMAN

LIONCREST
PUBLISHING

Copyright © 2019 Tracy Litt
All rights reserved.

WORTHY HUMAN
Because You Are the Problem, and the Solution

ISBN 978-1-5445-0400-1 *Paperback*
     978-1-5445-0399-8 *Ebook*

WORTHY HUMAN

BECAUSE YOU ARE
THE PROBLEM
...and the SOLUTION

TRACY LITT

CONTENTS

I dedicate this book to my unparalleled mother, Toby Litt.
I feel you with me every step of the way.

Your passing taught me to honor life. To show up fully,
to live with intention, and go boldly toward my dreams
while simultaneously teaching me to not take it too seriously,
to be present and grateful because it's only life after all.

I love you, Mom.

Acknowledgments

I feel deeply fortunate to have the abundance of love and support that I do. And it is with endless gratitude that I honor and acknowledge...

My wonderful dad, Jeff, who raised me to always remember who I am, for consistently being there for me, and for giving me such a kick-ass last name.

My incredible husband, David, whose support, patience, and love throughout this process have been everything an author could ask for.

My amazing teenage daughters—Taylor, Maddy, and Zoe—who were always there with words of excitement and encouragement while being cool with Mom tucked away writing in her office for hours.

My magnificent sisters, Barri and Jamie, who are the other parts of my soul and outwardly share their belief in me to anyone who will listen.

My awesome family and friends, who are incredibly supportive and excited about my work in the world.

My phenomenal community of worthy humans who show up and hang out with me day in and day out, learning, loving, and growing.

My talented book coach, Marie, whose guidance and support enabled me to bring this to life.

My sweet dog, Sunny, who laid at the bottom of my feet for hours while I was writing.

And to all the pioneers of personal growth that have come before me, who are my mentors and teachers. Whose work has paved the way for my work in the world. Tony Robbins, Marisa Peer, Byron Katie, Michael Neill, Jim Rohn, Jack Canfield, Brené Brown, and Dr. Joe Dispenza . . . to name a few. Endless admiration and appreciation to you all.

~

Hello, beautiful soul,

You're here and I couldn't be more excited!

I wrote this book for YOU. I wrote this book because I need you to know that you are enough, that you are worthy. And not because of anything you do, but simply because it is inherently who you are.

Your worthiness is your birthright. You are enough, you always have been, and you always will be.

It doesn't matter what your background is, where you grew up, what you had or didn't have, what traumas happened to you, who your parents were or weren't, if they were married or divorced, if you had too much love or not enough. You are enough. Period. End of story.

When you accept this truth, when you believe in this truth, everything changes. You are no longer seeking validation outside of yourself; you are no longer tolerating attitudes and behaviors that are all motivated by trying to feel like you're enough. You can be you, stand in your power, unconditionally love and accept yourself, and live a life based in choice because nothing is an indication of your enough-ness.

As a worthy human, you wake up and start your day automatically enough and deserving. You opened your eyes today, boom! You're enough.

The term worthy human hit me like a lightning bolt.

As I grew more and more aware of my own tendencies and behaviors and witnessed and observed the behavior and ways of being of so many around me—friends, family, clients . . . humans—a theme and pattern emerged.

My observation ultimately was deduced to this: there is the camp of "It's fine, I'm fine, I don't need to say anything, stay small, shrink down, don't rock the boat."

Or the pendulum swings all the way to the extreme opposite camp of being condescending, demanding, aggressive, defensive, and using an overassertion of power.

Both camps are driven by the same theme, in different directions— not feeling enough or trying to assert yourself into being enough. Neither option is necessary, fair for you, or healthy to your well-being and life.

Ah, but there is a space. There is a space in between, and I am claiming it as a WORTHY HUMAN.

Because in truth, that is what we all are. And when you know this, accept this, believe this, everything changes because you change.

You start to view yourself, your life, the world through the lens of I AM ENOUGH. It is from this place that everything you ever hoped, dreamed, wished, wanted, and prayed for can be reality.

A worthy human embraces imperfection, unconditionally loves and accepts themselves, possesses ease and confidence, knows what they are and are not available for, uses their voice, says no easily, says yes happily, puts their relationship with themselves on the top of the list, is a master of their mind, sprinkles playfulness and levity, understands they are responsible for everything that is happening in their life, and knows that none of what's happening is a reflection of their enough-ness, so they own their shit. They welcome being the problem and the solution because that's the only way to get where they want to go.

There is never a need to shrink or to puff your chest because you're already worthy. So you can simply express what needs to be expressed and ask for what you want, for what you need.

You become untouchable. You possess ironclad belief in yourself.

Worthy humans foundationally live in an entirely new way. You live, create, and experience your life through real empowerment based in your power of choice. Because you get to choose . . . everything.

And that's where our journey together will go. Into a new way to live, into understanding and realizing the depth and breadth of the choices you have, many that you don't even know you're making or may not have ever realized were choices in the first place.

This book will not only awaken you to new theory, perspective, and insight, but it will also provide opportunities for you to apply what you're learning to create tangible transformation. I call these opportunities "The Work" because taking action is everything.

Nothing changes if nothing changes.

Come on, my magnificent friend; let's get this party started.

XOXO,

Tracy

Choice #1

ARE YOU READY TO

Understand

HOW YOU BECAME THE PERSON YOU ARE?

"You are not responsible for the programming you picked up in childhood. However, as an adult, you are one hundred percent responsible for changing it."

—KEN KEYES JR.

Have you ever wondered how you became the person you are? Have you thought about how you developed your unique qualities, your beliefs, and the essence of your personality? Have you questioned why you respond or react in certain ways? Have you felt frustrated with yourself because you know you're stuck in areas of your life but you can't quite figure out why?

How did you become "you"?

It's the art of questioning that allows us to begin the journey of choosing to make a change.

We can choose to make a change in any area of our lives. Right now. Just by making a choice. If you don't start to question, you'll never change. It is only through curiosity and decision-making that you will be able to discover more about yourself and make changes in order to be your best self.

Even as a little kid, I was extraordinarily curious. I was always asking "Why?" I questioned the rules, I questioned everything I was told, and I always wanted to know why things were the way they were. It was fun for me, but now that I'm a parent, I have an understanding of just how annoying that must have been. Sorry, Mom and Dad.

The art of curiosity led me down this path of personal development, so my relentless questioning has become my secret to success.

I was in my late thirties when the gnawing curiosity became too much for me to ignore. As I started on my journey of personal growth, I realized that in order to go forward, I would have to take a look back at my life. You're going to have to do the same thing. You might not enjoy everything you review, but today is a new day, and you can make a new decision.

Throughout my life, I have been the "go-to" person, the advice giver. I'm comfortable in that role, I love helping people to see what's going on for them and talking through possible resolutions. As a kid I was comfortable in the company of adults where the conversations had depth and meaning. I always knew there was "more"; I just didn't know what "more" was or how I was supposed to find it. My mother taught me to own what was going on in my life through her actions in the face of adversity. She was a spiritual healer in her final years; she had chosen to take a path of personal growth when she was diagnosed with cancer. She wanted to examine what was going on inside her body, to find herself and heal herself. It wasn't enough that she was learning for her own benefit. She wanted to share what she was learning, so she wrote articles and became a speaker. I might have unintentionally picked up where she left off.

Like a lot of people, I didn't wake up to the truth until years later. Sitting at my desk in corporate hell, the gnawing within me became too much. I didn't want to half-ass my life. I could always get another corporate job, but what if I reached the end of my life and I hadn't followed my heart? Hadn't really gone for it? Sure, I was scared, but that's just fear. I could love fear and make a different choice, couldn't I?

I questioned everything. I wondered why the gnawing had suddenly got to be too much and why I had managed to ignore it for so many years, but more importantly, I wondered what I was going to do about it.

I hope you're ready to get curious. I hope you're ready to take a look back so that you can move forward. I hope you're ready to accept certain truths about how you have become the person you are today.

When I say accept, I do not mean that you have to condone anything that has happened in your life; I simply mean that you need to accept that it was or it is. To change anything in your life, you must be ready to accept what has happened and what is happening. Acceptance is your acknowledgment that something IS, without judgment or analysis. You are not denying it, ignoring it, or fighting against it; you are simply accepting it.

Play along with me and imagine that it's the day of your birth. Yay! Happy birthday to you, and welcome to the world! You are born into this universe a yummy, pure, delicious, worthy baby human. You are born totally. Fucking. Awesome.

You are born worthy. You are born lovable. You are born enough, totally enough.

Then you start to grow, you mature, you start living your life. The days, months, and years tick by, and life happens all over you, all around you. As life is happening, you are learning, being raised, creating meaning, and embedding beliefs into your subconscious mind.

Now, before we go any further, what do I mean when I say that you are a worthy human?

Your worthiness is your birthright. It does not come with conditions. It does not fluctuate. It cannot be measured against anything outside of you. It cannot be measured against what you do or don't do, what you have or don't have, what you say or don't say. It cannot be measured by what others say or don't say about you. It cannot be measured by anything that has happened to you. Your worthiness, your value, is yours automatically, and its existence as part of who you are is nonnegotiable.

The thing that has been a block to accepting your worthiness and something that will weave in and out of our journey together is your mind. Your mind is always working for you or against you. There's an entire chapter dedicated to your mind, but to understand how you became who you are today, let's start here:

You have a mind that consists of your conscious and subconscious.

Your **subconscious mind** is responsible for all of your effortless, yet vital, functions. It's responsible for ensuring that you breathe, blink, digest your food, remain at your optimum temperature, and it keeps your heart beating regularly. It also stores all of your memories and experiences, and it unquestioningly holds onto everything that you have learned. It doesn't decide what is good or bad; it just does as it's told and stores everything. It becomes a program that automatically runs behind the scenes.

Every day, Jen promises herself that she'll work out, eat well, and drink water. She knows that she needs to do these things because she's tired, overwhelmed, and struggling to maintain motivation, even for the things she loves. There's nothing "wrong" in her day-to-day life. She's just not following through on her promise to herself that she knows will help her feel better. She finds herself working late, so she can't make the gym class she wanted to go to. On her lunch break, the unhealthy option appears on her plate, and she has to have one more coffee to see her through the day.

Jen's choices are being directed by a subconscious mind that has unquestioningly stored beliefs of not feeling good enough and of not feeling deserving of taking care of herself. She feels like she's making a choice, but in reality, her behavior is being driven by her subconscious mind, which is the opposite of what she knows she really wants to do.

Your subconscious mind is matching everything you have stored with the thoughts, patterns, and behaviors you are experiencing today. It makes everything you say and do align with your self-concept, which is why understanding how you became who you are is a big deal.

Your **conscious mind** is responsible for logic, reasoning, and decision-making. It's intentional and it controls your actions. Through your five senses—sight, smell, sound, taste, and touch—it identifies incoming information, and it evaluates that information and decides on the appropriate action that needs to be taken. It's the part of your mind that you're aware of.

It's cold, wet, and dark outside. Lauren has been working at home all day, and she's comfortable, warm, and wondering if staying in to watch a film would be a more enjoyable way to spend the evening than what she had planned. She was supposed to be going for a run. It took a series of conscious decisions to get out of her front door and running. Get changed. Choose the playlist. Pull on the deeply attractive reflective jacket. Find those damn running shoes. At first, it's choice after choice. Lauren doesn't have to give it a second thought as the conscious choice is aligned with her self-concept, and it's just what she does on a Thursday!

Although it may seem that your conscious mind is running the show, it's not. Not by a long shot. Your subconscious mind is your blueprint for life, and it is the part of your mind that's in charge. Ninety-five percent to ninety-seven percent of your daily experience is coming from your subconscious mind, and only three percent to five percent is coming from your conscious mind. Surely that means we need to be more aware of what is being stored in our subconscious mind, right?

Without taking control of what we're storing, we're taking a back seat in our own life. We're being driven down a path that is based on historic experiences and old programming.

If we can take an audit of our subconscious mind, we can begin to understand how we got to this point in our lives. We need to audit our memories, our beliefs, our lived experiences, and the information we have learned. During the audit, we'll no doubt find stored data that is no longer serving us, and in accepting that, we have a choice to make. Do we still save a space for it in our subconscious mind, or do we move forward by making new choices and changing the programming? We can do that. We can choose what we store. Remember that our subconscious mind just does as it's told and matches our daily experience to what it's comfortable with. You can store whatever you want so that your subconscious drives you to the destination of your choice.

Imagine your subconscious mind is an elephant. Stay with me. An elephant stored with thirteen thousand pounds of beliefs, experiences, memories, invisible rules—your programming. No matter how adamantly your conscious mind wants something, without the alignment and agreement of your elephant, you'll get nowhere. That thirteen thousand-pound elephant is in charge.

Jason was an only child; he spent most of his childhood alone in his room. His elephant was filled with the belief that he didn't matter, that he was better off out of the way. As a young man starting his career, he was told he lacked initiative and drive. He was in a constant struggle to be a leader and use his voice. He wanted to improve and change, but that elephant just wouldn't budge.

To get that elephant to begin changing direction, you must begin to identify and change your core beliefs.

I'm not saying it's easy. It's not. This is the start of your journey, and you're doing an amazing job at changing the direction of your elephant already. By picking up this book, you have nudged it. By opening the book and starting to read, you have nudged it a little bit more. You're starting to and will continue to identify your limiting beliefs, and soon you'll be making new choices that will serve you and train your elephant to move in the direction you want to go.

Your conscious mind might be excited and ready to lose weight, but your subconscious mind believes your weight keeps you safe, so there you sit in front of the TV with a pint of ice cream, so you won't lose weight.

Your conscious mind is ready to start the dream business, but your subconscious mind believes you're not deserving of success, so you won't take action.

Your conscious mind declares you are ready to attract the love of your life, but your subconscious mind believes that you're not a lovable person, so you'll stay single.

That's the power of the subconscious mind. I don't know about you, but I'd rather have that power working FOR me rather than against me.

So, how did you get here?

As a human, one of our innate skills is our ability to create meaning. We assign meaning to things based on the experiences we have, the feelings we have about the shit that happens to us and around us. You, my fabulous friend, are a meaning-making machine. As a baby, a toddler, a kid, a teenager, and even as a young adult, you don't recognize the meanings that you are creating and how deeply disempowering most of them are to your adult self.

Jack is four years old, sitting on the kitchen floor, playing with his younger sister, Ellie, while their mother prepares breakfast. Ellie snatches Jack's toy, which leads to a minor tantrum and a lot of tears from Jack, who immediately hears, "You need to learn to share" from his mother, closely followed by a smack. That leads to more tears and another shout of "Stop crying, you're not a baby."

Jack's Meaning Maker: Crying is bad and something only babies do. I am not a baby; therefore, I must be bad, and I shouldn't cry.

Addison is five years old and experiencing the breakdown of her parents' marriage. The family is all still living together, so Addison hears every argument. She listens as they fight about money. It's always about how much money they don't have, how much one of her parents has earned, and how much the other parent has spent. Addison spends most evenings alone in her room, trying to drown out the shouting, wishing her parents would notice her.

Addison's Meaning Maker: Money sucks. It makes people fight. I don't like money.

———

Natalie is a typical seven-year-old, enjoying recess, wandering around the school playground when she spots a group of girls from her class playing together. "Can I play?"

The group turns to look at Natalie in silence. The girl in charge then shouts, "Get away from us; we don't want to play with you," as the rest of the group echo her words and carry on shouting as Natalie runs away from them.

Natalie's Meaning Maker: There's something wrong with me, I don't matter, and I'm not good enough. If I was good enough, they would want to play with me.

These three children have already created meanings that could potentially stay with them forever. They have attached meanings to situations that they have found themselves in, and those meanings have been stored in their subconscious mind. They have become part of who they are, forming the foundation of their automatic programming.

This is exactly what happens. We move through life creating meanings that become our core beliefs.

Your core beliefs inform how you see yourself, other people, and the circumstances you find yourself in. They inform how you think, how you act, and how you behave. Your core beliefs become invisible rules, which determine the way you live your life. Then, one day, BOOM, you become your adult self.

Because you were never taught to question these rules, you blindly assume the identity that has been created over time. That identity is *who* you are. You can only see the world through the lens of who you are. Your WHO is everything.

Jack believed that crying was bad, and he is now a parent himself. He suppresses his emotions, feels that it would show weakness if he expressed himself, and he feels disconnected from his wife and children. He found himself telling his young son that "real men don't cry," and even though he saw the hurt and confusion in his child's eyes, he didn't know how else to communicate with him.

Addison became a woman who works hard but struggles to save any money. As soon as she earns money, it evaporates. She dreams of running her own business but is stuck in a low-paying job, unable to see a way out. She resents people who earn more than she does, and her relationships are suffering as a result. She argues with her partner about money and feels as if her life is defined by her lack of money.

Natalie threw herself into her studies, pretending as she was growing up that she didn't want to do the things other girls her age were doing. On paper, she became a huge success, running a large company and earning more than any of her peers well before her thirtieth birthday. During the day, Natalie is the epitome of success, but when she goes home, alone, nobody sees her coping with anxiety and haunting thoughts that the people she works with don't like her, that she isn't good enough to be in that role, and that her self-confidence is at an all-time low.

These three adults haven't questioned what's happening in their lives. They have accepted that it's who they are and they're doing the best they can with what they have. Why would they question that?

As adults, we often don't realize that changing parts of ourselves, changing parts of our lives as we know them, are real options for us. Instead, we intensify our identity. We walk around thinking and saying, "It's just the way I am."

I'm here to tell you that is bullshit.

YOU are an outrageously powerful being that can change. You are a being that was made to grow and evolve. You can let go and break up with parts of yourself that don't serve you. You can change the parts of your life that don't align with the life you desire.

You can learn how to become aware, how to think differently, how to feel better, and how to develop new attitudes and behaviors. You can experience the kind of life that you don't need to escape from. You can experience a life you love.

You are malleable. You are not fixed. Isn't that exciting? When I discovered and learned this, I was beside myself: "Like, no way? This is fucking amazing. Why doesn't everyone know about this?" Which is a huge part of why I wrote this book.

The truth is that it was recently, recently as in a few decades ago, that neuroscientists discovered that your brain is not fixed. It used to be believed that the brain develops during a critical period in childhood, and then whoever you are as an adult is simply "just the way you are."

In this incredible, life-changing research, neuroscience has concluded that the brain continues to change throughout adulthood. Which means you can choose to think new thoughts and create an entirely new way of thinking.

Mind-blowing. Literally.

Every human in this universe deserves to know that they can feel, be, do, and create anything they deeply desire. Period. Anything that is coming up in your mind right now that is resisting this truth is totally normal. By the time we're done hanging out, you will believe and understand it fully.

So let's dig a little deeper into the truth bomb I just dropped.

From your time in the womb as a baby in the third trimester through to about seven years old, you are basically a video camera that is turned on and recording twenty-four hours a day, seven days a week, three-hundred-and-sixty-five days a year.

Get that; imagine your mind recording everything that is happening in your environment. I mean everything. All of that information is getting stored in your subconscious mind without any analysis or consideration for what it may or may not do to affect you. It's not optional; it's science. It just is. As you grow beyond seven years old, you continue to store memories, experiences, and self-created meanings, building on those that formed the foundation of your subconscious mind.

Remember I mentioned earlier that your WHO is everything? Well, this is how your WHO is developed.

As you're recording everything, your meaning maker is working overtime. Remember that as a human, you are a meaning-making machine. As every situation occurs throughout your life, your mind must assign it a meaning so that you can make sense of it and store it in the right place.

The issue with this system is that as a child, you had no idea that you were even creating meanings in the first place, and you definitely didn't know that those meanings could end up screwing you over in your adult life. As a child, you were not responsible for what happened to you or the meanings you created as a result. However, as the adult you are now, it is your responsibility to decide whether you want to change the things that are getting in your way.

Little Tracy's Meaning Maker

This is a great place to tell you about some of the meanings my little Tracy created, so you can see that we all do this. We are all influenced by our meaning makers, and we all have a choice, as adults, to keep those meanings or to change them.

I was born on May 15, 1977. It was a beautiful day because I came into the world. I was born with a birthmark on my nose that looked like the outline of a tree, and I remember my mom always told me that it represented my strength and power. It was lovely of her to try to make me feel better. A few days after I was born, my nana came to meet me in the hospital. Obviously, I don't remember this; this was the story I was told, but my internal video camera was turned on, right? Right. So, Nana comes in, picks me up to hold me, looks at my mother, and says, "Well, they can't all look like Jamie!" Jamie is my sister; she is two years older and apparently much cuter.

I know, who would say something like that? Don't get me wrong, I loved Nana like crazy, may she rest in peace. I know that she loved me too, but that love wasn't represented by what came out of her mouth, as was captured by my video camera.

Growing up, the inferiority I felt in comparison to Jamie became my very own elephant. There's a home video, taken by our mother, when I was only about four or five years old. Jamie was brushing her magnificent, shiny, long, princess-like hair with a beautiful silver hairbrush. The camera pans around the room and finds me sitting in the corner with a pick that I couldn't get out of my crazy, short, curly hair. I still get emotional when I watch that video. I can see the anguish in my eyes, looking across at my sister and absorbing a message that for her, life was effortless, while for me, it was a struggle. She was so good, but it was different for me, which must mean that I'm not as good.

Jamie's excellent grades would be effortless too. I would work so hard and still not get the answers right. Of course, that meant I wasn't as good as Jamie. As a child, I hadn't realized that the two-year age difference between us would be a factor, and I compared myself to my sister as an equal. I found it impossible to live up to the standard I believed she had set. The more effort I put in, the more stupid I felt. My parents didn't make any such comparisons, but my meaning maker had all the power.

Then there was drama camp. Guess who was the star of the show and who was in the back row, making up the numbers in the general cast? Yup, you guessed right. If I had a dollar for every person who came up to tell me how amazing my sister was, I would have been as rich as a Hollywood A-lister. It was killing me slowly. I knew they were being kind and they were right, my sister was amazing, but it just became more evidence for me to store in order to prove that I wasn't enough.

The one story that I believe depicts every sibling's worst nightmare happened when we both wanted to be cheerleaders. Of course, Jamie was selected for the squad and was presented with her letterman jacket. I, on the other hand, was not selected for the squad and was made the team mascot. Seriously. My meaning-making machine was on fire that day.

It wasn't just my incessant comparisons to my sister that created meanings that would stay with me until adulthood. As a child, I had a daring streak, something I'm happy to choose to keep in my adult life. I was five years old when I decided to take a midnight stroll around the neighborhood with my best friend. While we were out having an adventure, little did we know that my parents had called the police, thinking that I had gone missing. Returning home, without a care in the world, I was greeted by two policemen who looked much less frightening than my mother in that moment. Rolling their eyes, they said, "See, they wander off, but more often than not, they come home within the hour. We'll leave you to deal with her." She certainly did "deal with me," and while I knew that what I had done was wrong, stupid, and naughty (because my mother told me multiple times), my meaning maker learned that I get attention when I do things that I'm not supposed to do.

All of those meanings became "me." They helped shape the person I became. As I lived through my adolescent and teenage years, I was a full-on rebel. If you said something was black,

I'd swear it was white. If my parents didn't want me to do something, it became my top priority. If a teacher said I couldn't do something, I did whatever it took to get it done. If only they had told me I couldn't do my homework. I didn't care about school because I didn't value my studies. I believed I wasn't smart enough to succeed academically, so I put my energy into succeeding in other ways.

I became the person that everyone would turn to. If a friend needed something, I was there. It didn't matter if it was day or night, I didn't question anything. I just did what I could to help. I needed the validation. I wanted to feel that I was enough. The only way I could do that was by trying to be everything to everyone.

These choices and behaviors were driven by my subconscious programming. I had stored my core beliefs, thanks to my meaning maker, so I knew that I received attention when I took risks. I knew that I wasn't good enough or smart enough, so my subconscious mind made sure my experiences reinforced those beliefs on a daily basis.

What's the Truth?

Well, none of the meanings I created were true. Not one. Through my own personal growth journey, I discovered everything I am sharing with you. I was simply being led by the meanings my little Tracy created out of those experiences, which in turn acted as the lens through which I saw the world and made decisions.

The truth is, if I want attention, I can give it to myself in healthy ways. I was and always am good enough, and I'm super fucking smart.

So, what do I mean by the lens?

Think about a pair of glasses. Glasses have a prescription. Your subconscious programming is the prescription in your lenses; therefore, you will only be able to see and create your world through that lens, through that prescription.

You will carry on looking through those lenses until you realize that you are not who you want to be, where you want to be, or feeling how you want to feel. That realization could come from a specific catalyst, such as a divorce, an illness, a significant loss, hitting a dead end in your career or business, or it could come from that gnawing feeling of "Is this it?"

If you're asking yourself, "Who am I and what's my purpose in life?" you are ready to change your lenses. If you feel that your life is stuck on a never-ending loop that is sabotaging your potential, it's definitely time for a new prescription.

You get to choose to change the prescription in your glasses. *The truth is you're choosing either way.* You're choosing to continue to be led by your subconscious mind, repeating your patterns and staying where you are, or you are choosing to identify your meanings and beliefs so that you can change them.

The super awesome news is that beliefs are simply thoughts you choose to think over and over again, making them real.

And you, my worthy friend, can choose your thoughts.

YES, you can change yourself and anything in your life that you want to.

My client Rachel was hitting a wall in her business. "I'm doing all the right things, but I'm just not making enough money," she told me during our first session together.

I asked her to finish this sentence: "Money is . . ."

The words poured out of Rachel in a tidal wave of anger: "Evil, hard to make, bad, the root of all my problems, the reason people argue, not something that grows on trees, the reason rich people are assholes."

"Where did you learn these things about money?" I prompted.

"My parents were always fighting, and usually it was about money. They were so mean to each other, and I think it was the reason they hated each other. I don't want it anywhere near me; it creates so many problems."

Rachel's meaning maker had been hard at work when she was growing up. It makes complete sense that if she believes that money causes problems, her subconscious will do everything it can to keep money away from her. Her conscious mind can try doing "all the right things," but her subconscious mind has all the power.

At one of my live seminars, Victoria explained that she was struggling in her marriage. "I'm not being negative about him," she was quick to say. "I know he loves me, and he would do anything for me, but I just feel alone and disconnected when we're together."

I asked Victoria what's stopping her from talking about how she's feeling with her husband. I saw her eyes drop to the floor as she replied.

"He works so hard, he's the provider, and when he gets home after a long day, the last thing I want to do is bother him with my shit."

There we go; I knew that was the work of a childhood memory. "That's interesting, where does that come from?"

"I just feel like my stuff isn't as important as his stuff," she whispered, sinking into her chair.

"Where did you learn that?" I asked.

It doesn't matter how many questions it takes; we have to find out where these meanings were created so that we can change them.

"Oh my God, my mother, oh my God." She began to cry. "My mother used to hold her shit in and not say a word to my father. Then, on my wedding day—MY WEDDING DAY—my mother said to me, 'Just remember to keep it together, talk to your girlfriends if you have to get stuff off your chest, but don't overwhelm him with your stuff.' Can you believe she said that on my wedding day?"

Of course I could believe it. As a general rule, people have no idea how powerful their words are. This was an easy message for Victoria to absorb, as it was handed to her by her mother after years of experiencing the message in their family's interactions. It doesn't get much more powerful than that.

Owning a large insurance company had ensured Nicole was at her wit's end. She was burning the candle at both ends and couldn't remember the last time she had a day off. Every aspect of her life was suffering, but she couldn't bring herself to slow down.

I didn't have to ask her anything at all. During one of our early conversations, Nicole told me about her father.

"My dad was an awesome provider. We had a great life, even though my mom would get frustrated that he wasn't around as much as she would have liked. He taught me that if I wanted to be successful, I had to keep working. He said that he didn't worry about not taking time off because the more he worked, the more he made happen."

There's nothing wrong with Nicole's desire to follow in the footsteps of her father, except that she had created an unnecessary obstacle for herself. Nicole could choose what success looked like for her. She could redefine what she wanted to "make happen" and channel her energy into more than work. She didn't have to create success in the same way her father did. And she didn't have to kill herself trying.

The Drip Process

Your programming doesn't just come from the meanings you have adopted. It is also made up of what is directly inputted into you through what you have been told and how you were raised. We can see this from Victoria's and Nicole's experiences. The direct influence through words and actions from your parents, siblings, teachers, guardians, religious leaders, extended family, friends, and coaches had an impact on your subconscious mind.

I call it the *Drip Process*. It's when someone drips their shit on you.

It's inevitable and generational. Your great grandma dripped shit on your grandma, your grandma dripped shit on your mom, and your mom dripped shit on you. It's now up to you to decide if you're going to carry on the cycle.

The Drip Process installs things in our subconscious mind that are both empowering and disempowering and is something that we must become acutely aware of.

It's important to appreciate that the generations that have come before us lived in different times, with different challenges, values, and expectations.

For many of our grandparents and great grandparents, stress and pressure were a nonnegotiable way of life.

Men were raised to be stoic; they were taught that showing emotion is weakness. They were told that the harder they worked, the more productive they would be, and therefore the more valuable.

Women were raised to remain obedient and subservient. They were told to be humble and not to burden others with their problems.

Universally, we are influenced to think that our worthiness and happiness are based on what we have, what we do, what we buy, the house we live in, how hard we work . . . the list goes on, and it is HOLY BULLSHIT.

Consider this:

- If you had the kind of mom who overreacted every time you fell down, can you see why you overreact or dramatize?
- If you were only praised when you were the best and criticized when you had a misstep, can you see where your perfectionism and overachievement comes from?
- If you were brought up in a family that was frugal and you have memories of your parents telling you that "money doesn't grow on trees," can you see where your money struggles originated?

- If your household fought a lot and you experienced extreme tension and shame, can you see why attaining a state of peace and calm is challenging for you, but treating yourself like shit and attracting relationships that do the same feels familiar to you?
- If you were brought up in a stoic family with the motto "Suck it up, buttercup," can you see why you might struggle to express vulnerability and emotion freely and with ease?

The beliefs you hold have been infused into you. The question becomes which beliefs are helpful and which beliefs are limiting you?

THE WORK
(The work works when you work it. 100% of the time.)

It's time for some self-discovery. Time to capture all the stuff and thoughts that have come up in you since you started reading. So, think about your upbringing, your childhood.

- What happened to you?
- How were you raised?
- What is blocking you from being who you want to be?
- What prescription might be in the lenses of your glasses?
- What inspired you to pick up this book?

Write down everything that comes up as a result of what we've talked about so far and these questions. When you reflect on what you wrote, you'll find some of your beliefs that have been holding you back interweaved throughout your words. This is just the start. Throughout our journey, you'll continue to identify more and more.

Here's the thing: if you stop and realize what I'm saying, you'll see that you are made up of subconscious meanings that you involuntarily created as a child, most of which are totally disempowering in your current adult life. You have received input from other people's beliefs and ideals that you, the true, consciously-creating-adult you, might totally disagree with. Just because your mom believes something or your religious leader tells you something is true, that doesn't mean it aligns with your personal truth.

You get to choose. This is YOUR life. Yours. Not theirs. Yours.

This is your personal life experience. You don't have to believe anything that you don't want to believe. You don't have to abide by any invisible rules that don't align with your true, unapologetic, worthy self.

I'm Jewish. I was raised Jewish. I have a real, living, amazing Christmas tree in my home every holiday season. I'm not supposed to though, am I? The world's rule is that Jewish people don't have Christmas trees. My rule is that I do what feels good for me. One of my favorite things in the world is that feeling I get when it's nighttime, my beautiful family is sleeping, the house is dark, and the lights on the tree are glowing. The smell of the fresh, living Frasier fir is in the air. The feeling brings tears to my eyes as I type this. It brings me joy.

Sure, are there people in my life who disagree? Yup. Are there people who have judgments and opinions about my choice? Yup. Does it bother me? Not even a little bit. Do I think twice? Not even once. Zero fucks given. I'm not being dismissive, callous, or bitchy. I'm simply honoring myself and the fact that I get to create my personal life experience based on what feels good to me and that the most important opinion in my life is my own. My life, my rules. Your life, your rules.

There is not one thing about who you are, your actions, your beliefs, your thoughts, your feelings, your behavior, or your habits that are permanent. Let me say that again and louder:

THERE IS NOT ONE THING ABOUT WHO YOU ARE, YOUR ACTIONS, YOUR BELIEFS, YOUR THOUGHTS, YOUR FEELINGS, YOUR BEHAVIOR, OR YOUR HABITS THAT ARE PERMANENT.

You can become aware of, and then shift and change anything. Yes, even those things you say that are immediately followed up with "That's just the way I am." It's not just the way you are unless you want it to be. Yes, really.

You are a limitless, delicious, worthy human, and YOU GET TO CHOOSE. Everything.

Your past does not predict your future. Who you have been up until this moment is zero indication of who you can be. The way you have experienced life can be instantly shifted through the choices you have available to you.

And that's the journey we're diving into together.

A journey of living from the inside out, a journey of personal power, a journey of choice, a journey of activating your limitlessness, a journey of living from the space of your inherent worthiness.

Repeat our **Worthy Human Mantra** after me:

I am worthy. I am enough. I am powerful. I get to choose.

Choice #2
ARE YOU WILLING TO
Own YOUR SHIT?

*When you think everything is someone else's fault, you
will suffer a lot. When you realize that everything springs
only from yourself, you will learn both peace and joy.*

—DALAI LAMA

Excuses, excuses, excuses. Do you have any idea how many
excuses you make on a daily basis? Seriously, have you ever
stopped to realize how many excuses pass through your
mind each and every day?

How many times do you justify and rationalize the reasons
you're acting a certain way, or why you don't have the results in
your life that you desire, or why you're in a bad mood? When
something goes wrong around you, do you ever stop to notice
how quickly you blame someone or something outside yourself?

"I don't have time to create my website. I'm so busy. Every time I try, I am bombarded with questions from the kids, emails, and the long list of things I should be doing."

"I would totally go to the gym if I could, but my husband travels. And the kids' schedule is so busy, I'm always rushing around. Plus, the gym I like is too far away."

"I know it's important to finish that program and hire a coach to help me, but I can't afford to do that. I don't have the money."

"I would have been promoted by now if my boss wasn't such a douchebag. He just doesn't like me."

"If I was twenty years younger, I'd go back to school and launch that business. I'm too old now, and I don't know how to start."

"Today was the worst; I'm so stressed. The traffic was insane; it made me so aggravated."

"I can't be visible in my business. The last time I made an offer, nobody hired me. My confidence hit rock bottom, and I haven't recovered."

The list of excuses for why you're not where you want to be in your life is endless. I'm sure you can easily make your own list in a matter of seconds.

Yes, you're the master of this. You're the master of staying powerless, of not owning your shit, of coming up with all the reasons why, of not accepting that anything is your fault.

There's nothing wrong with you; you're not broken. I promise.

We're not raised to understand our personal responsibility.

We haven't been taught how to own every result we have throughout our life. We haven't had lessons in taking responsibility over how we feel, over who we are being, over how we respond and what we do on a daily basis.

Until now.

Taking Radical Personal Responsibility is one of the key requirements of changing anything and everything in your life.

> Kristen is an entrepreneur running a busy digital marketing company. We began working together when she realized that she was burned-out and struggling with her lack of results. She was frustrated, unhappy, and starting to wonder if running her own business was too much trouble.
>
> "How do you take care of yourself?" I asked.
>
> "I don't have time. I race around all day, keeping the business going, and then as soon as I get home, I race around after the kids. I get into bed and my husband wants to have sex, so from the moment I get up in the morning, I'm prioritizing the business and my family."
>
> Every week, during our session, Kristen would set goals that she knew would propel her business forward. She was animated as she talked about them; she seemed excited to get started and hopeful about the results. Yet, the following week she would return deflated, having not completed the agreed-upon tasks.
>
> "I just didn't have time," she would say. "I'm not really a tech person,

and I didn't have time to find out how I could do it. I needed to talk with my accountant first, and I didn't have time to call her."

The list of excuses was getting ridiculous, and she could see the pattern repeating itself each week. During our fourth session, Kristen arrived with an edge to her that I hadn't seen before. She was sharp in her responses, and I wanted to know what was going on for her.

"I do everything. I am running the business by myself, trying everything in my power to grow it, so that my family can enjoy the benefits. I'm a chauffeur to the kids, and they barely mutter a word to me when we're together. I listen to my husband tell me all about his day, whether I want to hear about it or not, and I even muster up the energy to have sex with him. Nobody asks me what I need. I've had enough."

"What is it going to take for you to put yourself first?" I asked.

"It's fine; I know this is how life is when you're an entrepreneur. I have kids and a husband, so I know that frustration and pressure is part of the deal. It is what it is."

It wasn't the time to say, "You know that is bullshit, don't you?" So instead, I said, "It is what it is because you are choosing for it to be this way. You are choosing to be everything to everyone, and now you are resenting that choice."

Kristen burst into tears. Tears are good. They're a release.

"Oh my God, I'm doing this to myself."

Yes. That's the harsh reality. Taking Radical Personal Responsibility isn't easy, but it does open the door to a whole new world. For Kristen, that meant saying no to driving her kids everywhere and coming up with alternative options. She now takes the first thirty minutes of every day for herself; she plans her day, meditates, and starts her morning feeling prepared. She meets her girlfriends twice a month, has joined a yoga class, and says that she gets her best ideas after an evening of laughing with her friends or exercising. She takes inspired action on those ideas, and her business is booming. With her renewed energy and enthusiasm, she no longer sees time with her husband as a chore either!

Kristen embraced the fact that she was the only thing standing in the way of living the life she wanted.

Scott left a voicemail for me, asking if I could help him with his negativity and anger. I could have guessed that was his challenge from the tone of his message, and I breathed a sigh of relief when his voice softened at the end of message and he said, "Please, can you help me to get past this?"

From an outsider's perspective, Scott had a successful life. He was the director of his company, he shared custody of his two children with his ex-wife, and he was happy in a new relationship. He managed to mask his anger so that it didn't affect his work or his family, but it was driving him to a dark place when he was alone.

He called in for our second session together. He couldn't mask his fury, and before I had a chance to open the session, he started: "I hate her; she's such a bitch. I lost a huge deal this morning because of her. She always does this to me."

After some gentle breathing exercises, Scott was calm enough to talk about what had happened. I still had no idea who "she" was or what "she" had done.

"My ex-wife called me before work this morning. I was preparing for my presentation, and she dropped a bombshell about my kids. She makes all the decisions, and I don't get a say in anything. It pisses me off."

"What was the bombshell?" I asked, expecting to hear something that might have an impact on the time he could spend with his children.

"They're sleeping over at a friend's house tonight, and I don't know the friend or their parents."

"Oh." I was sure that there had to be more to it, so I asked, "Is this happening on her time or yours?"

"Hers," he replied, as if that was obvious.

"Do you trust your ex-wife's judgment about who she allows to look after your children?" I asked, wondering if I had missed a part of the story.

"Of course," he replied again, as if that was obvious.

"So, you can choose to let it bother you, or you can choose to let go of trying to control everything. That's a necessary practice for parents who don't live together, releasing control when you don't have your kids. You have shared that you want to get past your negativity and anger. Does holding onto control bring you closer to or further away from what you want?"

"Further away from what I want," he whispered.

"So who needs to take responsibility for losing the deal this morning?" I asked, wondering if he was ready to think about what had happened.

He hesitated. "Okay, okay, I get it. It's on me."

It wasn't easy for Scott to own that. It was much easier to blame his ex-wife and absolve himself of responsibility, but that would only have served to fuel his anger.

In that moment of freedom and realization, Scott had made his choice.

From there, it was much easier for him to become aware of how he had always been responsible for the way he responded to difficult situations. It's in the word, *response-able*, meaning you have the ability to respond. Scott even called his ex-wife to share his epiphany of ownership, and their co-parenting relationship improved dramatically.

As a result of this newfound awareness, Scott continues to be aware of himself. He continues to choose to look to himself and check in on what he owns in every situation before allowing himself to respond or react.

Nothing is a one-shot deal. Growth and change take consistency and choice.

You are able to choose how you respond.

Pretty fucking awesome, huh?

The truth, the actual truth, is that all of your excuses, justifications, and reasons are keeping you stuck, keeping you in a victim mentality, and keeping you powerless. If you are going to be able to access your limitless potential, it's ALL GOT TO GO.

And we begin right here, right now, with 100 percent ownership, Radical Personal Responsibility, because it is the foundation and basis for all of the other choices you will need to make. It is the foundation for claiming your power. It is the foundation for feeling how you want to feel, doing what you want to do, creating what you want to create, and being who you want to be.

- The reason you are not working out regularly is not because the gym is too far or because your kids have a busy schedule. It's because you're choosing to not make the time.
- The reason you haven't started that business isn't because there's so much competition out there and you don't know where to start. It's because you're choosing to give your power away to fear and letting your mind run you.
- The reason you don't prioritize yourself isn't because there isn't enough time and everyone else needs you. It's because you are choosing to put everyone else before yourself and you are choosing to not change that behavior.
- The reason that you're still in that job that sucks you dry and brings you no joy is not because you don't have an option and the job market is really tough. It's because you are choosing to settle, letting the fear of the unknown take over and not believing in yourself.
- The reason you're in a pissed-off mood isn't because your partner or friend is an asshole and they made you feel angry. It's because you're choosing to let it in and take it personally.

Let's clear this up right now and for the official record:

NO ONE and NO THING can MAKE you feel anything, ever.

It is your choice to allow it. It's because you created an interpretation of what happened or what was said and then chose to rub yourself down in it.

Maybe you're thinking, "That's great." Or, "That's bullshit."

Either way, keep reading, and I'll introduce you to the foundation of your personal power, or in more direct words, the path to everything you have ever wanted in your entire life.

Radical Personal Responsibility

Every one of these three words is significant. Significant in their own standing and significant because this one choice, this one principle of living, can single-handedly change your life right now.

RADICAL: far-reaching, thorough, complete, total, comprehensive, exhaustive, sweeping, wide-ranging, extensive, all-encompassing. I'm pretty sure that means EVERYTHING.

Seriously, everything. That means everything you are experiencing or not experiencing, feeling or not feeling, being or not being, doing or not doing, comes directly from you.

PERSONAL: It means total ownership. The agreement that anything that comes into your world, your life, or your day is there or not there due to something in you. Owning that you can make a choice over your actions, opinions, meanings, interpretations, thoughts, beliefs, responses, feelings, attitudes, and behaviors.

It means you are the problem and the solution. It means that in truth, the only thing standing in your way, the only block or barrier, is YOU. Which then means the way to unblock and remove the barriers is YOU. This is the best news ever! You don't have to wait on anyone or anything. You *ARE* you ... so, game on!

RESPONSIBILITY: As I said before, look at the word. *Response-ability*. Able to respond. You have the inherent ability to respond. Response is a choice; it's conscious. It's what happens when you're living in your power. Without it, you're reacting. Reaction is what happens when we are living from the past. Living from our default. When we are not choosing. When we are not conscious.

It's super normal to be in shock about this. I get it: right now you might be feeling scared, a little annoyed, and very curious about what Radical Personal Responsibility can really do in your life.

Once you have let the shock wear off, you will awaken to the greatest sense of freedom you have ever experienced. The freedom of knowing it's all you, for you. It always has been, and it always will be.

You are the problem and the solution, the obstacle and the answer, the pain and the relief.

I know, it's fucking incredible. It's the foundation of experiencing a powerful, wondrous, beautiful, joyful, successful, and fulfilled life.

All of those reasons, all of those justifications and excuses, haven't served you. The cold hard truth is excuses are lies we tell ourselves so nothing has to be our fault, so that we don't have to be responsible or own our shit. Because if we did . . . if we did, we'd have to step up and be the solution. We'd have to take action or take a good, deep look at what we really want, and that's unfamiliar. Your mind doesn't like unfamiliar. Yes, we'll dive deeper into that later on.

The more I stepped into my Radical Personal Responsibility, the more my clients stepped into theirs. If you're not living in Radical Personal Responsibility, you're not really living.

For me, the most powerful thing about stepping into 100 percent ownership was becoming untouchable. I take full responsibility for how I feel, what I let in, what I choose, how I show up, and being my full, vibrant, real take-me-or-leave-me self! I practice it, moment to moment, day in and day out. Everything is my choice, and that means I eliminate all of my bullshit, and you get to do this too.

If I'm not at my fitness best, it's not because I'm too busy or I don't have time. It's because I'm not making the choice to make it a priority.

If I'm dragging my feet on launching a new idea or program, it's not because I don't know how. It's because I'm choosing to not take action because I'm choosing to give my power away to whatever BS I'm making up about it.

If I'm impatient and reacting to my kids, it's not because they suck. It's because I'm allowing myself to react rather than choosing to pause, breathe, and choose my response.

If I'm annoyed and feeling disconnected from my husband, it isn't because he's an asshole. It's because I'm allowing myself to focus on whatever one thing rubbed me the wrong way rather than choosing to look at all the wonderful things about who he is.

Are you getting this? Good. Because it's everything. When you choose Radical Personal Responsibility, you choose empowerment. You choose choice. You choose freedom.

When you don't choose Radical Personal Responsibility, you are being influenced and affected by what happens in your external world. You are as happy and as valuable as the last thing that happened outside of you. You are a victim of your circumstances. Yuck. This makes you completely dependent on everything last perceived as good or bad that happened. You live a life underpinned by "Look at what happened TO me" rather than "Look at what happened FOR me." That one shift changes everything.

Embracing Radical Personal Responsibility is the highest level of freedom you will ever have.

Empowerment

One of the things I hear the most from people is the need and desire to feel empowered, to live a life of empowerment. We want to be stronger, more confident, and to feel the freedom, strength, and courage that comes with all of that.

Radical Personal Responsibility is the real basis of empowerment. You cannot achieve empowerment without choosing a life based in it.

I want to take a moment here and get super clear on what empowerment actually is. Through the work I do in this world,

I have created a new definition for empowerment that makes it crystal clear…

To consciously and consistently access your power of choice to align with what serves you.

Fabulous, right? To be empowered, you must be conscious and aware, you must be consistent and accept that every single thing is based on your ability to choose, and the way you make these choices is all based in what aligns with what will serve you. As soon as you know how you want to feel, who you want to be, what you want to do and create in this world, you can choose the path that will take you there.

Empowerment isn't "hear me roar." Empowerment isn't a destination. You don't simply become empowered one day and then you're done and empowered forever. It's a journey. It's a moment-to-moment, day-to-day, choice-by-choice way of living. And it's fucking incredible.

And without your best friend, Radical Personal Responsibility, empowerment is unobtainable. To change your life, you must know that you are the root cause of ALL you experience. Knowing this, rather than allowing outside forces to trigger old patterns, is the source of your power.

The other operative word in all this is CHOICE.

The power of choice is everything. There is not one thing that doesn't fall directly under your power to choose. As we continue this journey, you will be in awe of how many amazing choices you get to make and how they create every experience you have in your life: every feeling, every action, every frustration, everything. What you tolerate is a choice. What you allow is a choice.

Yes, you read that correctly. What you tolerate and what you allow is your choice ... just in a more polite, less obvious way.

The word *allow* means to give someone permission to do something.

The word *tolerate* means to allow the existence of, accept, or endure something. It has the word *allow* in the meaning so, clearly, they are in the same club.

It's easy to use those words and release yourself from owning your shit, from believing you are choosing it. But don't kid yourself: it's still a choice.

Choosing Radical Personal Responsibility is like flipping a switch—from victim to claiming your power, from blame to ownership, from stuck to free. Ahhhhhhhh ... it feels so good!

And please understand, I'm offering you an option, an invitation that requires you to choose. If you are unwilling to make this choice and try it on, then you won't get any further. You will stay exactly where you are, doing what you're doing, feeling how you're feeling, experiencing what you're experiencing.

THE WORK

Take a second. Pause from reading and ask yourself:

- Do I wake up every day feeling happy and grateful? Really feeling happy and grateful?

- If I rate the areas of my life on a scale of one to ten, with ten being absolutely amazing, where do I fall out?
  - My relationship with myself
  - My health and wellness
  - My love life
  - My family
  - My business/career
  - My money
  - My fun and enjoyment
- How many hours a day do I spend feeling agitated, negative, and "meh"?

Quite frankly, I want more for you. I know you do too. You're an amazing, worthy human, and you deserve the yummiest, most satisfying, fulfilled, glorious, joy-filled life you can possibly imagine. Yes, you DESERVE. If there is any part of you that feels resistant to this, you won't by the time you're done hanging out with me. Because the TRUTH is you deserve everything you can imagine, everything you desire, everything you crave, and everything you envision for yourself. You deserve it because you are enough. Because you are worthy. Because you are a human being. Period.

Stress, Conflict, and Resistance

One of the most incredible benefits of Radical Personal Responsibility is what happens with stress, conflict, and resistance. We experience stress, conflict, and resistance regularly throughout our lives. They are all part of the human experience. You may have believed that there's very little you can personally do to impact or shift their power, until now.

Stress. Stress. STRESS. The silent killer. Stress is the response that keeps your heart rate up, that keeps you overwhelmed, that constantly releases cortisol throughout your body, that congests your mind and soul, and that breeds physical disease.

Your mind is connected to your body, so when you're thinking stressful or negative thoughts, those are the thoughts that trigger your stress response and keep you living in chronic stress. Your system is constantly releasing cortisol as a result of these thoughts because your brain doesn't know what's real and what is only in your mind. A threat is a threat as far as your mind is concerned, whether it's self-induced or not. The continuous stressful thoughts mean that your body never gets to rest or return to homeostasis. This, in turn, creates an inner environment that easily breeds disease and lowers your immunity; it affects your blood flow and causes illness. And it makes you easily triggered and reactive.

There are other significant factors that rest within your soul and have power within your body. If you're feeling disconnected, holding on to resentment, suppressing your emotions, or not practicing forgiveness, there's a blockage. Those feelings don't have anywhere to go, and that energy congests inside your body. I'm sure you'll agree with me when I say that's not a healthy environment in which you can thrive.

Of course, not all stress is bad, and there are moments of benefit, specifically with short-term bursts of acute stress. Like when you hear about a mother finding the strength to lift a car to save her child. Short-term stress can aid in focus and mental acuity, and it also assists in physical performance. The problem is that so many of us are living with chronic stress, stress experienced over such a prolonged period of time, that you may not even recognize what it feels like to not be under stress because you've been living with it for so long.

Have you ever slept on a brand-new mattress after ten years of sleeping on the same old one? You wake up the morning after your first sleep on the new mattress, and you are stunned to realize how shittily you'd been sleeping for so long. Exactly. It's time to get off your shitty stress mattress. It's time to take responsibility for your stress levels and treat your mind, body, and soul with respect. Stress isn't happening to you. You are responsible for your stress.

Conflict. Not all conflict is bad. We have an association with conflict that leads us to think it means anger, negativity, or that we won't get along with others. In reality, conflict just means that two or more people have different opinions.

We make the notion of disagreement quite terrifying, but it's not at all. We don't all come out of the same movie theater and have the same opinion about what we've just seen. What's stopping us from having a soul-driven conversation rather than an ego-driven conversation? What's stopping us from listening to someone else's opinion, without judgment, and being relaxed about the fact that sometimes the only resolution is to agree to disagree?

If we perceive conflict to be negative, we descend into a bad place very quickly when we find ourselves in the middle of a disagreement. This can be hell on our relationships. When you live your life based in Radical Personal Responsibility, you are able to choose to see conflict as constructive. You are able to own your shit and create a connected experience through listening, not trying to be right, and allowing both the other person and yourself to be heard. To really take responsibility for the conflict you are experiencing creates an entirely new level of communication and connection.

Resistance. Resistance is the refusal to accept something or an attempt to prevent something. When you don't want a certain outcome, you can become resistant to it, or push against it, if you will. This creates the opposite of Radical Personal Responsibility.

The more resistance you have toward something, the more the thing that you resist will persist.

If you resist feeling your fears, they will become louder and bigger. If you resist your emotions and shove them down, they will grow bigger and become a more prominent issue. If you resist not taking 100 percent ownership, the problems you are experiencing will get more challenging and more pervasive.

Inherently, in not taking ownership, you are resisting. Not choosing to take Radical Personal Responsibility actually perpetuates stress, conflict, and resistance in your life.

One of my clients, Penny, had been struggling with anxiety and chronic stress for years. She tried everything from medication to therapy in an attempt to start enjoying her life. When we started working together, the first thing we worked on was her relationship to her anxiety. What Penny realized was that she was seeing the anxiety as something outside of herself. She believed that the anxiety was something that was happening to her.

That belief was causing intense resistance, which only served to feed the anxiety more and more, increasing her levels of chronic stress.

Penny made a choice to take Radical Personal Responsibility. She pulled her anxiety toward her. She wrapped her arms around it. She owned it. She accepted it (she didn't condone it, just accepted its presence), and through doing that, she broke her resistance to it, which allowed her to make different choices. As a direct result of owning the anxiety, she was able to start healing herself.

I recall a specific moment when she was being called to present at a conference for her company. This would have been a situation that previously would have kept her paralyzed or asking for extra Xanax. Instead, she was able to accept, love, and calm the anxiousness. Through Radical Personal Responsibility, intentional breathing, and consistently telling herself, "I am enough. I see you, anxiety, I've got you, and I love you." She was standing in front of her peers giving a presentation like a boss! All because she took responsibility for it, and when you do that, you realize how much power you have over these "things, problems, or ailments." You are able to step into your power and realize that you are more powerful than anything when you make the choice to own it.

I had a similar experience with resistance. My resistance and my fear of change were keeping me stuck. (I have a whole section on fear for you later on, because it's that important.) Fear used to be paralyzing for me. Fear of the unknown, fear of success, fear of failure, fear of being good enough. You name it, I feared it. It's funny, even as I write this, I am smiling and laughing because none of those things are real for me anymore. Ah, the freedom that comes with taking Radical Personal Responsibility!

Anyway, I'll get back to the point. It took me over two years to take the leap from the comfort of my cushy corporate America job and dive into the world of entrepreneurship. It took me awhile, but I finally realized that it was because of fear. I was afraid of failing, afraid of the unknown, afraid of rejection, and even afraid of success; yup, that's a thing. I overcame those fears by owning them. I stopped resisting them. That started with a choice.

I made the choice to not give my power and potential away to fear. At the time, I saw fear as this beastly thing that sat in opposition to me; it sat outside me. I saw it sitting across the table, daring me to try and challenge its power. Then I made a choice and Radical Personal Responsibility stepped in. I owned it. As soon as I did that, everything changed. Its power was gone, and the power was now mine.

As soon as you take complete ownership, you can choose differently. You diffuse it. Through your personal power, you lose the resistance and you place yourself in the seat of choice. When I say bring it to you and claim it, I actually mean literally bring it to you.

THE WORK

Visualize the feeling or the situation that you are resisting. See it sitting across the table from you. Now, put your hands out and bring it toward you. Sit it right down on your lap. It's not nearly as scary now that it's sitting with you, is it? Talk to it. Say to it, "I see you, I feel you, and I love you." How do you feel about it now? Through that small series of choices, you can take your power back. It's simple, yet profound!

Radical Personal Responsibility enables you to claim your power. You can live in a daily state of empowerment. It is the road to being completely untouchable.

What does it mean to be untouchable? It means you are unaffected by any circumstance or event outside of you. You don't give your energy away. You use your voice easily and effortlessly. Your opinion is the sole opinion that matters. You aren't responsible for how other people respond or react. You don't believe everything you think. You own your shit. You stay in your own lane. You are the love of your life.

So, is it time? Are you ready to stop giving your power away to everything and everyone outside of you? Are you ready to become untouchable?

How to Take Radical Personal Responsibility

It starts with a choice, funnily enough, as everything in life does. It's time to make a conscious choice to own your shit and to live a life based in Radical Personal Responsibility.

THE WORK

- Are you ready to shine a light on your excuses and personal bullshit?
  - Grab a piece of paper and draw a vertical line down the middle of the page.
  - On the right side, write down everything you want. I mean EVERYTHING. Think about all the different areas of your life as you're doing this.
  - Then shift to the left side and write down all the reasons why you don't have that right now or why you are not taking action toward it.
  - It'll look something like this:

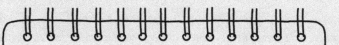

WHY I DON'T HAVE IT:

- I don't know how. Clients are hard to find. There are so many people that do what I do.

- There's never enough time. I'm so busy. I'm so easily annoyed and triggered.

- It sounds nice but I have no energy by the time the day is done. I just want to sleep.

- Money is not easy to make. I hate even talking about it.

- I don't have the time or money.

- The kids' schedule is packed. When I'm done working, I drive them around, then its time for dinner, bed, all that shit. Not enough hours in the day.

WHAT I WANT:

- More clients in my business

- Be calmer and spend more time with my kids.

- Have more sex with my husband.

- Make more money

- Travel!

- Go to the gym, so I can have more energy and lose 20 lbs.

○ Can you see where you need to take Radical Personal Responsibility in order to live your best life?

· We are going to have a lot of juicy conversations about the power of language later on; however, I want to give you a powerful word shift that will help you tremendously as you decide to take Radical Personal Responsibility.

- ◦ Replace the word "can't" with the word "won't." It might feel like a small shift, but trust me, it's life changing.
- ◦ Using "can't" allows you to remain powerless. It tells your mind that it's not possible, so your mind moves on to the next thing that it needs to deal with.
- ◦ When you use "won't," the next natural step in your mind is to question why you won't. Then from there, you automatically start a new chain of events.
- ◦ Instead of saying, "I can't make it to the gym this evening," say, "I won't make it to the gym this evening." That's interesting. Why won't you make it to the gym?
- ◦ Try it on; be prepared to be shocked by what's really stopping you.
- • When anything happens in your life, from an argument with your spouse to feeling frustrated with your child, from not taking action in your business to not prioritizing yourself, instead of looking outside of you, look inside yourself for ownership rather than outside of yourself for fault or blame.
  - ◦ Ask yourself, "What is happening within me that is creating this experience?"
  - ◦ Ask yourself, "What new choice can I make that will bring me closer to what I want?"

When you choose Radical Personal Responsibility, you say yes to a life of freedom, you say yes to a life based purely on your power of choice. You say yes to yourself.

Repeat our **Worthy Human Mantra** after me:

I am worthy. I am enough. I am powerful. I get to choose.

Choice #3
ARE YOU READY TO
Wake Up
AND BECOME YOUR OWN OBSERVER?

"No problem can be solved with the same level of consciousness that created it."

— ALBERT EINSTEIN

There's so much going on. It feels like we don't have time to take a breath. It never stops. Our senses are being bombarded with information twenty-four hours a day, seven days a week.

It's coming at us from all angles—the media, our partner, our family, our friends, our colleagues. It's circling around us and being absorbed by us all the time.

There's no escape; we have access to anything and everything, instantly. The advancements that we're experiencing in technology continue to be both beneficial and detrimental.

Technology is hugely beneficial when you can have a video

chat with your best friend who lives on the other side of the country, watch your niece grow up and not miss a thing even though she lives eight hours away. You can have virtual business meetings with ninety-nine people from thirteen different countries all at once. You can order a pair of sneakers or your entire grocery list and have it delivered to your doorstep at a time of your choosing. You can buy a car that will park itself. You can start an online business, share your mission and message reaching millions of people with the click of a few buttons. You can be in a conversation with a stranger, trying to remember the name of the hot actor in the latest blockbuster, and pick up your smartphone and have the answer in a nanosecond. That's just scratching the surface of what's available to you, and I haven't even gotten started on the cute baby and animal videos.

It's detrimental because it doesn't stop. It never stops. Access to information has become an addiction, and the constant stimulation is too much for us to cope with. We're spending more time with our heads down, distracted by and sucked into these tiny screens, than we are spending with real, human people. We're lost in a world that doesn't exist. It's a world of perfect photos, perfect lives, and we can't live up to the comparisons we make. We are losing the ability to "just be." Our desire for connection is falsely satisfied, so we're more disconnected than ever. We are no longer in tune with our creativity, our imagination, and who we are in the real world.

The nonstop access to information and the on-demand culture that we live in has made it even more critical than ever to pause on purpose, look up, and become aware.

At times it can feel like we're doing life like a zombie with a checklist. We're totally unaware, simply going through the motions.

Yuck. You deserve more than that. We all do.

> Amanda woke up every morning, rolled over, and reached for her phone. She scrolled through the perceived perfection in her friends' lives, she was bombarded with quotes about how she's perfect just as she is, while feeling far from perfect, and then she invited the world's problems into her bed as she read the latest news. Before she realized the time, the kids would be running around the house, and thanks to the foul mood that the day's news had put her in, not to mention her neighbor's perfect holiday snaps, she was shouting at the kids to get ready for school. Running late, as always, she found herself in traffic, gesticulating to other drivers and then snapping at her assistant before she even made it to her office.
>
> There was never a moment for Amanda to pause. She had become a victim of her habits. It wasn't until she became aware of her morning routine that she realized how unaware she had been. It was time for her to make different choices so that she could honor herself through the way she started her day.

No one is going to make you create space. No one is going to come and knock on your door to shut down your devices and outside stimuli and force you to experience more presence in your life. No one is going to make you stop, breathe, and raise your awareness. Only you can choose to do this.

Without awareness, without raising your consciousness, there's no chance of changing. It is impossible to change something that you are not aware of, and you cannot become more aware without slowing down, creating space, and observing yourself and the world around you.

What Is Consciousness?

That is something that is still being studied and examined as we evolve. However, for our journey together, consciousness is simply the quality or state of your awareness—awareness of yourself and your environment.

You must first be aware in order to make new choices about how you want to feel and how you want to behave.

THE WORK

I have four questions for you, and I'd like you to take some time to think about your answers. It's only through allowing ourselves the time and space to become aware of what's going on in our lives that we can choose an alternative path.

1. Describe how you felt when you got out of bed this morning. Were you excited about your day? Were you worried about your day? Were you indifferent about your day?
2. What is something you want to take action on but haven't? What's stopping you?
3. What was the last thing you ate, and why did you choose that to fuel your body?
4. Where are you right now? Look around and take in your environment. How does the space make you feel?

This is an exercise you can do throughout the day. Get to know your body. If you repeatedly feel tension in the same part of your body, choose to explore that and take action to improve your well-being. We're aiming to raise our awareness of every aspect of who we are.

Awareness is a requirement for growth. Period.

Without awareness of all aspects of your life, you are zombie-like, moving through life on autopilot. The really sad thing is that you don't even realize it.

Kelly had a lot going on when we started working together. She had dangerously low energy levels that resulted in her being impatient and reacting in ways that she felt she couldn't control. She felt guilty about her behavior, chastised herself as a result, and the cycle had become increasingly damaging. As a mom of three, the wife of a prominent surgeon, an entrepreneur, and a friend to anyone who needed help, she certainly had a lot of drains on her ever-depleting energy.

Kelly personified the "zombie checklist." She went through the motions day in and day out. She had become so used to the daily cycle that she couldn't see the triggers and became angry before she had time to recognize the signs.

"I'm a bad mother, I shout at the kids, and I get frustrated with my husband for not being more available, but I knew that when I married him."

Kelly was oblivious to the reasons why she was behaving in ways that weren't in congruence with her values.

We started with Kelly observing herself and keeping a journal of her triggers, her commitments, her tasks, and her habits. Through that work, we could see the details of her daily routine, of the situations and people that triggered her. We noticed that most of her days were spent doing things that she felt she should do, not doing the things she wanted to do that would support her vision of being a loving mother, a supportive wife, and a successful entrepreneur.

Kelly chose to slow down and create space. She learned to take a moment to breathe and to ask herself what she was doing and why she was doing it. She learned how to raise her self-awareness and do self-inquiry when she wasn't feeling the way she wanted to be feeling.

That space allowed her to make different choices which, in turn, started to change her life. Change her energy level. Change her relationship with herself and start living her vision.

Raising Your Consciousness

When you choose to raise your consciousness, you literally wake up to who you are and you find out what has been getting in your way.

Before we go any further, I've got something I'd like you to try. This will show you one way of raising your awareness about your body. It's something we can often ignore, but the more we get to know every aspect of ourselves, the more conscious we become.

THE WORK

Take a deep breath and right here, right now, make a promise to yourself. Repeat after me: "I am going to practice awareness and make choices that allow me to become the observer of my life because that which I cannot observe, I cannot change."

Now (once you have read the instructions because you can't read with your eyes closed, right?), close your eyes and take a few deep

> breaths. Slowly scan your body. Where do you feel tension? Where do you feel tightness in your body?
>
> Focus on that part of your body, and breathe into that space. As you're breathing, allow yourself to let go, allow the tightness to relax.

We are so caught up in our routines and our habits that we don't even attempt to venture outside of what has become our "normal."

Here's a wonderful little parable shared by writer David Foster Wallace, which explains consciousness beautifully. He imparted this brilliance during his commencement speech to the Kenyon College class of 2005.

There are two young fish swimming along in the ocean. An older fish swims by them, headed in the other direction, nods at them and says, "Morning, boys. How's the water?" The two young fish swim on for a bit, and then eventually one of them looks over at the other and goes, "What the hell is water?"

I imagine you're thinking, "Well, I'm not a fish, so how does this help me?"

I would like you to challenge your own status quo.

If you feel that you lack confidence, maybe it actually has more to do with the way you talk to yourself. If you change the way you talk to yourself, you could increase your confidence in a heartbeat.

If you feel sad and triggered a lot of the time and describe yourself as a pessimistic person, maybe it's due to your attachment to the past. If you chose to practice forgiveness and place your focus and attention on what's good, you could be immediately happier and more optimistic.

Your lack of self-confidence or your pessimism could become your "water." It could be so familiar to you that you no longer question it or recognize it; it is just part of your identity. I'm here to tell you that you can call BS on any parts of your identity that aren't working for you. As soon as you become aware of it, you can choose to change it.

Whatever level of consciousness you are currently experiencing, we are going to raise it because if you're not aware of it, then you can't do anything about it.

Becoming Your Own Observer

The more you raise your consciousness, the easier it becomes to be your own observer.

When I first started my personal growth journey, I would walk around with two versions of myself. Stay with me.

As I walked, I would imagine a hologram version of myself walking beside me, watching me, observing me, and offering feedback on what she saw. Hologram Tracy would say, "Whoa, was that a judgment?" when she heard my internal dialogue respond to someone or something I had seen. She would ask, "Did you mean to order extra fries with that?" when she knew I was having a bad day and turning to comfort food. She would question me when I was feeling frustrated, "Why did you snap at your

74

husband? He was only trying to help," and she would remind me, "I think it's time to pause and consider why you're doing what you're doing and consider what's going on inside you."

She helped to remind me that in order to raise my consciousness, I needed to observe myself all of the time. She also helped me to see when I was honoring myself: "Yeah, nice work on being relaxed while your kids were arguing; you calmed that situation like a pro." Hologram Tracy helps me to see the behaviors that I need to keep as well as the behaviors I need to change. She helps me be in awareness of myself and honest with myself. You can borrow her or create your own version, whatever works for you.

Your observer can see you roll your eyes when your boss makes a request; they hear you form judgments about the women around you; they notice that you complain with frequency; they observe when you're deliberately busy so you don't have to acknowledge your emotions; they witness you disregard your commitment to exercise. Believe me: you need your observer to help you see what you have allowed to become second nature. Your observer helps shine light on your blind spots.

THE WORK

What would your observer have seen so far today? What would they help you to become aware of that you have ignored or considered "normal" up until now? What would be "your water"?

Making the choice to be your own observer and raise your consciousness means increasing your self-awareness so you can feel better, live better, and be better.

Curative Consciousness

The coolest thing about raising our consciousness is that our new level of awareness can be curative in itself. Just by noticing something that we're inadvertently doing, we can immediately rectify the behavior and, in doing so, feel much happier.

I was running a workshop, which is one of my favorite ways to serve and reach people, when I heard Sarah talking to her peers about how let down she was feeling by her mother-in-law.

"All I need is support, but what I get is a disapproving look and unhelpful comments. Last night, I was trying to help my toddler get to sleep, and my mother-in-law walked past the bedroom saying, 'Are you really going to say no to another story?' Yes, after fourteen stories, it was time to say goodnight. Just as my son's eyes were closing, she shouted, 'Is he asleep yet?' which was followed two minutes later by 'Are you going to let him keep crying like that?' Seriously, the woman could be a little bit more supportive, right?"

I could hear the disappointment and frustration in her voice, and while I didn't disagree that Sarah's mother-in-law could definitely work on her volume and timing, there was more to it than that. We talked about the origin of her disappointment, and it was as if a lightbulb had been switched on behind Sarah's eyes.

"I expected her to be much more accepting of the way I choose to raise my son. She raised a wonderful son; I should know, I married him, so I thought she would be an ally. After all, she must know how hard it is to raise a son, mustn't she? I have never talked to her about raising children, though; I just assumed."

"Great work, Sarah. Huge awareness. So, what's really causing your frustration?"

"I'm frustrated because she's not living up to my expectations. I can't believe I have never had a conversation with her about this."

Sarah became aware of the origin of her frustration and letdown. Boom. Curative. Now that Sarah was aware, she had choices.

So she made the choice to talk with her mother-in-law. They talked about the trials and tribulations of raising a son. They laughed, they shared stories, and they drank a lot of wine.

Sarah set herself free. Her awareness was curative.

How Conscious Are You, Really?

The higher you raise your consciousness, the more power you have to choose and create the life you desire. When you start to raise your consciousness, you will notice what's happening on the inside with your feelings, emotions, and attitudes. The more conscious you are, the more aware you are, the more mindful you are, the more perspectives are available to you. Simple, right?

THE WORK

I know that you're familiar with social media, so let's imagine that you're scrolling through the day's updates and you get triggered. You spot an entrepreneur. Their message is exactly what you need to hear, they're showing up being unapologetically who they are, and based on their following, you can see that their business is booming.

Then, you notice a shift in your own energy.

You feel the dip, the shift in yourself.

Rather than getting dragged into a spiral of "Why are they doing so well and I'm not?" or "I want to be doing that, I want to be my authentic self!"

I would like you to try a different response, a mindful response.

Take all of the emotion out of it, and notice what's happening.

Scan your body and find the areas that have experienced a shift in energy.

Get curious about your response without judgment and without an opinion; just notice it.

What have you become conscious of?

What were your thoughts, what were you telling yourself in that moment when you felt that shift, that dip in yourself?

What is the honesty of what you were experiencing?

Maybe the honesty behind the shift in energy is a belief that you aren't good enough. A deep doubt of whether you will ever get to the level of success you want. A feeling of inadequacy or isolation.

Now you are in awareness. Now you can choose differently.

You can choose to breathe deeply and shift your focus into how far you've come. Into how many people you have helped with your business. Into meeting yourself with grace and compassion and removing yourself from comparison.

When you make a new choice, you create a new experience.

It's the daily responses that we experience on autopilot that can lead us down a path that we probably wouldn't choose to take if we were making a conscious decision.

THE WORK

Think back over the day so far. How many times can you remember experiencing a disempowering state? Have you felt angry, frustrated, disappointed, or overwhelmed, to name just a few? How many observations did you make about your behavior when you were experiencing those states? Allow me to ask:

- Have you been agitated at all today?
- How much space have you created so far today?
- What was the first thing you did when you woke up this morning?
- Have you stopped to appreciate something and connect with a sense of gratitude so far today?
- Has there been anything you wanted to do today that you haven't followed through with?

If you spend a significant amount of time experiencing disempowering feelings each day, not creating space for yourself, and not connecting with the things that will help you move forward, it is an indication that you are operating at a low level of consciousness. That means that your thinking and awareness are limited. With a low level of consciousness, it will be challenging to make choices that will help you to make positive changes.

When you are raising your consciousness and functioning with a high level of awareness, you will experience a greater ability to access your power of choice consistently. You will be living in your higher self and, as a result, experience the empowering states and feelings of joy, happiness, compassion, kindness, creativity, and confidence, just to name a few.

Your higher self isn't concerned with ego. It is the zero-fucks version of you. It is the version of you that you dream of becoming, the version that is ready and waiting to show up in the world.

You don't need to be superhuman in order to choose to live consciously. It's simply about being aware of yourself and making consistent choices. You have the power to do that in every situation you find yourself in.

IT'S STORY TIME. SAME GIRL, SAME SITUATION. COMPLETELY DIFFERENT EXPERIENCES.

Jessica raced home from work to prepare for her first date with a new romantic prospect. She's not getting her hopes up because internet dating hasn't worked out for her so far.

"Nobody tells the truth online, do they? This young, marathon-running project manager will probably turn out to be a geriatric janitor who couldn't run if he was being chased. There's no way that a guy that cute would want to date me. I suppose that could be a picture of his grandson?"

The ping from the phone cut through Jessica's thoughts. Reaching into her bag to find her phone, she found herself hoping her date had cancelled; instead, it was a message to say that the restaurant had moved their reservation due to an admin error.

"Great, now I've got an extra thirty minutes to spend worrying about whether I'm meeting a serial killer."

With her clothes laid out on her bed, Jessica ruled out each and every outfit, one by one.

"That one makes me look like I should be at a job interview, that one makes me look like the job interview is at a strip club, that one makes me look like my mother dressed me for a job interview, and that one, wait, that's what I was wearing for my last job interview. Ugh!"

Taking a shower, Jessica visualized meeting her date for the first time. After her last dating disaster, her best friend told her to visualize the first meeting so that she could confidently walk in to the restaurant knowing that whatever happened, she's got this.

"Maybe he will be the guy in the picture. Cute guys could be serial killers too, right?"

Having decided on a not-too-interview-y looking outfit, Jessica stood in front of the mirror, looked herself up and down and thought, "That'll have to do."

On that inspiring note, she reached for her car keys, knocked them off the shelf, and lunged forward in an attempt to catch them.

"For fuck's sake. I've broken my toe," she screamed at the keys as she clutched them so tightly they imprinted into the palm of her hand.

Looking down at her bloody, stubbed, but unbroken toe, she decided that this was a sign from the universe that she shouldn't go out tonight. Or ever.

Still muttering to herself about what a bad idea this was, Jessica started her car. It took approximately twenty-three seconds before she had forgotten all about her toe and was concentrating only on the asshole driver who had pushed his way in front of her, making her miss her turn because she was focused on giving him the one-fingered salute with an aggressively timed beep of the horn.

Having decided that all men were serial killers who shouldn't be allowed to drive, Jessica arrived at the restaurant, thrilled to see a male member of the staff waiting at the valet service.

"Like I'd trust you with my car."

After parking her car in her own indomitable yet imprecise way, Jessica marched into the restaurant like a woman possessed.

Now, let's assume that Jessica's date wasn't a serial killer but was a lovely, honest guy who was looking forward to meeting an equally lovely woman for what he hoped would be a great first date. Meeting Jessica's lower-self might not have been what he was expecting. This probably wouldn't have been the version of herself Jessica would have chosen if she had been more aware of how she was allowing the evening to progress.

Let's try again. Welcoming Jessica's higher self.

Jessica raced home from work to prepare for her first date with a new romantic prospect. Having recently had a couple of dates that didn't work out, she had high hopes that this one would be different; this could be the start of something special.

"Nobody tells the truth online, do they? This young, marathon-running project manager might not be exactly who he says he is. Well, that's fair enough, it's not like I made my most recent selfie my profile picture. I can't believe a guy that cute actually wants to have dinner with me. Whatever happens, this is a great way to start the weekend."

The ping from the phone cut through Jessica's thoughts. Reaching into her bag to find her phone, she found herself wondering if her date had cancelled; instead, it was a message to say that the restaurant had moved their reservation due to an admin error.

"Great, now I've got an extra thirty minutes to spend relaxing in a bubble bath. That's a much better plan than having a quick shower. This evening is already going my way."

With her clothes laid out on her bed, Jessica quickly decided on the perfect outfit.

"That one makes me look like I should be at a job interview, that one makes me look like the job interview is at a strip club, that one makes me look like my mother dressed me for a job interview, and that one, wait, that's what I was wearing for my last job interview. They gave me the job and I've never been happier, so that's now my lucky outfit. I'll just ditch the jacket for this evening."

Soaking in the bath, Jessica visualized meeting her date for the first time. After her last date didn't have the happiest of endings, her best friend told her to visualize the first meeting so that she could confidently walk into the restaurant knowing that whatever happened, she's got this.

"There he is, exactly like his picture. He's cute. Wow, he stands up as I walk toward him, kisses me on the cheek, and, wow again, he smells amazing."

Having decided on the lucky outfit, Jessica stood in front of the mirror, looked herself up and down, and thought, "I'll be honest, I'd date me."

She reached for her car keys, knocked them off the shelf, and lunged forward in an attempt to catch them.

"For fuck's sake. Please tell me nothing's broken," she pleaded with her keys as she clutched them so tightly they were imprinted into the palm of her hand.

Looking down at her bloody, stubbed, and thankfully, unbroken toe, she decided that this was a sign from the universe that her prayers had been answered.

"Nothing broken, phew. Let's see if any other prayers get answered tonight."

Still nattering to herself about how lucky she was, Jessica started her car. It took approximately twenty-three seconds before she had forgotten all about her toe and was concentrating only on the driver who had pushed his way in front of her, making her miss her turn because she was focused on what must have gone wrong during his day that had made him so impatient.

"I hope you're okay," she thought, wondering if he was rushing to get home because of a family emergency. Maybe it was good news, maybe he was about to become a father!

Having decided that tonight was a good night to have prayers answered, no matter how fast you're driving, Jessica arrived at the restaurant, thrilled to see the valet service was available.

"Thank you for looking after my car," she said, walking into the restaurant with a spring in her step.

Come on...which Jessica would you rather meet for a first date? Which Jessica would you like to BE on a first date?

The Glass Elevator

Someone I deeply admire in the personal growth industry, Michael Neill, gives an incredible explanatory tool in his book *The Inside Out Revolution*. This is my brass tacks interpretation of his creation.

Imagine we each live our lives in our own glass elevators. Your elevator goes up and down. The lower the floor that your elevator is on, the lower your awareness is. Your thinking is limited, and as a result, you experience low-level moods and feelings.

The higher your elevator goes up, the higher your awareness is. Your awareness is raised, allowing you to experience higher-level moods and feelings.

Imagine that you're in your glass elevator, hanging out on level two. Right in the middle, almost eye-level to the happenings of your life. Right in the middle of your shit. Your stressors, your perceived problems, the argument with your spouse, the frustration from your children, the overwhelm from your business, the fight with your ex. From level two you are only able to see things equal to what they "seem." You remain in your limited perspective, in what's familiar to you.

What if you don't want familiar? What if the way you feel hanging out on level two isn't the way you want to feel?

Well, my friend, all you have to do is make a choice.

Choose to press the elevator button and take yourself up to level twenty-nine. *Going up.*

As you travel in your glass elevator, taking you up, up, up, further away from level two, what do you think happens?

If you said, "I'll see things differently. I'll have greater perspective. I'll be less connected to what's happening and more able to access my power of choice," then great job! Because you are totally right.

Imagine life on level twenty-nine. Now, this is more like it. There's lightness in the air, a joy-filled existence. There's no place for ego or judgment here. It's a peaceful place, somewhere you will be supported, encouraged, and accepted just as you will do the same for others. On level twenty-nine, you have endless choices.

By pressing that elevator button, you have lifted yourself out of your own way. Yes, it is as possible and as fabulous as it sounds. All you need to do is choose.

Breathe

I can't talk about raising consciousness without a conversation about what I believe to be the single most powerful tool available to you. Not only is it completely life changing, but it is always available to you, and it won't cost you a dime. The only thing you need to do is choose it. I know—fucking amazing.

BREATHING.

Breathing on purpose and with purpose is the most powerful tool you have at your disposal. It is available right now to support you to live an empowered, incredible life. I love breathing on purpose so much I tattooed the word *breathe* on myself.

What makes breathing so unquestioningly powerful?

When you change the rate, depth, and pattern of your breathing, you send new signals to your brain. You interrupt your nervous system; you interrupt yourself. In that moment, you have created the space to choose what you would like to do next.

When you were born into the world as this delicious, totally awesome baby, you had a deep, slow, steady pattern of breath. As you grew up and life happened, your breathing became more shallow, erratic, and rapid. It happens to all of us.

And right about now, you just became aware of your breathing. Perhaps you took a deep breath or yawned. As a direct result of that, you will feel a bit calmer, a bit more aware. See, it's magic! Not really, it's science, but it's magic science!

You might start to notice that you breathe erratically, or in some moments, you don't breathe at all. You know what I'm talking about. When something goes wrong around you and you actually hold your breath. When you get physically hurt, or when you are waiting for important news, you stop breathing. Or conversely, when you get nervous, your breathing might speed up. Now that I've brought this to your attention, you will start to become aware of it.

Breathing on purpose helps bring about a profound level of awareness because you are slowing yourself down. You are literally interrupting yourself by interrupting your nervous system and sending new signals to your amygdala.

What the hell is an amygdala? Great question.

The amygdala is a small, almond-shaped section of your primitive brain that is responsible for your emotions, survival instincts, and memory. Survival instincts meaning the flight, flight, or freeze response that occurs when you're experiencing stress, a threat, or fear.

These new signals that you've sent to your brain thanks to breathing on purpose support the amygdala in calming down, slowing down, and creating some space from the stimuli it was experiencing. This is where the magic begins. It is that moment, when you intentionally slow down, that you are able to connect with yourself, raise your consciousness, and make a choice.

When we pause and breathe on purpose, we have the experience of presence. The power of awareness. We connect with the wisdom and goodness of our souls. In the calm, we gain clarity. We drop out of our heads and into our hearts. Weslow down. We see with new eyes and hear with new ears.

We become aware of our own motives. We see our own truths and desires. We place ourselves in the seat of choice.

Breathing on purpose, breathing consciously, is life changing. You can practice it as a part of a daily ritual or intermittently throughout your day. Or both.

Breathing on purpose is an essential tool for habit change.

Let's say you've made a new decision to follow healthy eating habits. When you notice yourself feeling the compulsion to eat something unhealthy, pause and choose to breathe on purpose. You'll interrupt the behavior and create the space you need to move away from compulsion and into conscious choice.

Perhaps you've made a decision to be calm and not go straight to losing your shit with your kids. When you notice yourself feeling heated, feeling your body starting to pull you into default freak-out, pause, and choose to breathe on purpose. You'll interrupt yourself and create the space for a new choice.

Becoming aware of your breathing will connect you to yourself and slow you down. In doing so, you will increase your awareness of yourself, your thoughts, your attitudes, and your behaviors.

Let's Get Technical

We talked about the fact that technology can be both beneficial and detrimental at the start of this chapter, but let's get real. We need less screen time and more sun time. Period.

What does that mean? Tech detoxes and more nature?

Well, yes. It's time to implement tech detoxes from your phone, tablet, TV, and laptop. If you're choosing to raise your consciousness, then you're choosing to experience being present.

At first, it might feel like you're losing a limb, but I promise you'll be okay and then you'll be better than okay.

I recently spent a beautiful weekend with my family for my father's birthday. There was a lot of rejoicing, happiness, love, and reflection. We spent time together. I mean together, not just sitting in the same room attached to our own phones.

This came about because I declared a phone detox. That meant my teenage kids, yes, *teenagers*, did not have their phones. I kept mine on airplane mode, so I could take pictures but not be disrupted or distracted. My kids checked and double-checked to make sure I was sticking to the rule, which I was.

Yes, of course my kids rolled their eyes when I declared that there would be a phone detox, but they got over it. This exercise allowed me to show them what connection really is, what it means to engage and be present. If we don't teach them this, they're never going to learn. As adults, we need to remind ourselves of this and lead by example.

Life is not meant to be half-lived from behind a screen.

If you're not behind your screen, you can choose new things. You can take a walk in the grass with bare feet. You can grab a book, *this book*, and read outside with the sun on your face. Take a moment to look out of the window and notice the trees swaying and the birds flying. When you are in nature, when you are present, you are building your observer muscles. Your consciousness is being raised.

Join the Consciousness Revolution

We're evolving. We're beginning to understand and embrace our limitlessness, our potential, our ability to change, and guess what? You can choose to begin your own consciousness revolution right now.

We know that we are not fixed beings. We can change, we can grow, and we can let go of the parts of ourselves that don't serve us.

None of those changes are possible without raising your consciousness, so are you ready to become your own observer and join the consciousness revolution?

Before you do anything else, you have to choose to become more aware. Decide that you want to raise your consciousness so that you can experience and create the life you desire and deserve.

THE WORK

- Commit to breathing on purpose as an intermittent daily practice. And yes, this is the same practice of breathing on purpose I recommend you use, in the moment, to interrupt yourself and shift your behavior.
  - Set a reminder in your smartphone to go off four times a day. This reminder needs to say something that you will honor, like "Stop, love yourself, you have time, and BREATHE." There really are benefits to technology, and ironically, this is one of them.

- ○ When the reminder goes off, do three rounds of flagpole breathing. Simple, right?
- ○ I call it flagpole breathing because I imagine a flag being raised up a flagpole, waving at the top, lowered down to the bottom of the pole, and held at the bottom before it goes back up again.
- ○ Here's how you do it: take a deep breath in for a count of four, hold your breath at the top for a count of four, exhale for a count of four, hold at the bottom for a count of four, and then repeat. Visualizing the flag helps to stay in the moment.
- ○ The important thing is to always do three consecutive rounds and do not rush. Count silently and slowly: one Mississippi, two Mississippi, three Mississippi, four Mississippi for each phase.
- · Wake up like it's 1985. Do not, under any circumstances, roll over and pick up your phone when you wake up. When you do that, you immediately focus on other people instead of focusing on what your immediate needs are. Make the first twenty minutes of your morning all about you.
- · Remember your glass elevator. Choose to travel to level twenty-nine as often as you want to. Choose it when you aren't feeling how you want to feel. When you need a different perspective. When you need to shift and feel better. I use this one on the regular. As soon as you realize you're on level two, visualize yourself in your glass elevator and say, "Going up!"

We are going to spend more time concentrating on our feelings and why awareness of them is so critical. For now, start playing with these exercises, and you'll be ahead of the game!

Raising your consciousness is powerful. When you choose to

raise your consciousness, you start to grow, to heal, to feel better, to connect to yourself and everything around you. You are able to help yourself get out of your own way.

Repeat our **Worthy Human Mantra** after me:

I am worthy. I am enough. I am powerful. I get to choose.

Choice #4
ARE YOU READY TO RUN YOUR MIND, INSTEAD OF IT RUNNING *You?*

"We live in the feeling of our thinking,
not in the feeling of our circumstances."
—MICHAEL NEILL

We've all heard the platitudes: "Change your thoughts; change your life," "Mindset is everything," "What you think is what you create." Each one is true, but not entirely helpful. They don't tell us HOW.

Fear not, my friend, that's what I am here for. You can call me the Platitude Whisperer. I am about to unravel the truth, and you are about to realize just how fucking powerful you are.

Before we go any further, I need to tell you something. It's important, so you need to concentrate. Okay, here it is: you are not your mind.

I'll say it again; come in closer: YOU ARE NOT YOUR MIND.

Take a deep breath and let that land. I fully understand that none of us were taught this essential truth when we were growing up, so it's brand-new information. Why weren't we taught this? Sit tight... that answer is coming shortly.

If you have resistance to this information, I get it. It's a new conversation for most people. If you're thinking, "No way, my mind is crazy, it never stops, I'm constantly overthinking everything and doing what my mind tells me to do, so how am I NOT my mind?" That's okay; you're not alone in responding that way.

Regardless of how you define your mind, crazy or otherwise, the only thing you need to know right now is that YOU ARE NOT YOUR MIND. Period.

You are a human being. *You knew that already, right?* As a human being, you are made up of cells, atoms, and molecules, all of which are energy. The reason that energy matters so much when we're learning about the mind is because every thought you have is also energy.

Now that we're clear that you're a human being (*you're welcome!*), we need to get just as clear on what you possess due to your status as a human being. You have a head, an arm, a leg, to name just a few of your possessions. You have them. You are not your head, you are not your arm, and you are not your leg.

You HAVE a mind. You are not your mind. YOU ARE NOT YOUR MIND.

You can direct whether you nod your head, wave your arm,

or kick your leg. I need you to realize that you can also direct your mind.

I know. It's fucking incredible. And it's the complete truth.

When you choose to accept and embrace that you direct your mind, not the other way around, then everything changes. EVERYTHING. Choosing not to embrace this will keep you stuck and powerless, a victim of your own existence. And pardon me, but fuck that. Life is too long and too short.

Mastering Your Mind

Mastering your mind, which I also refer to as your human technology, can raise you from level two to level twenty-nine in an instant. *Remember our glass elevator?*

Mastering your mind is mind magic. Nothing will ever make you feel anything ever again. Knowing that you are not your mind and you are the director of your mind allows you to be unfuckwithable. It will give you the highest sense of freedom you've ever experienced.

So, if this is the way it is, why didn't we know this when we were growing up? The answer is *neuroplasticity*. It's a big fancy word to explain that your brain is malleable, it is not fixed. That means that you can change it. Yes, you can change your mind.

Imagine an Etch-a-Sketch. You can write something on it, then erase it and start over. Even if that Etch-a-Sketch has been in your basement for twenty years, and you don't believe that the writing will ever disappear, it magically does, and you have the space to write something new.

Neuroplasticity is a relatively recent discovery. Luckily for us, we now know that we can upgrade our human technology.

Right about now, you're probably getting excited and with good reason. You can change. You can change your mind! I don't mean that you can change your mind about ordering Chinese food and choose pizza instead (although it's fine by me if you do); I mean that you can actually rewire and change your mind. WOOP WOOP, let's hear it for neuroscience.

At the moment, when you feel like you're being directed by your mind, it's because you have familiar thoughts that you're so used to thinking you don't question them. They're like a familiar route home; you know it so well that you haven't stopped to think about if there's a quicker route or a more scenic route. You unquestioningly follow the same path home every day. Your mind is packed full of familiar routes for your thoughts; some of them serve you well, but some do not. You haven't questioned them; they just automatically start their journey and follow the same path each and every day.

You have already chosen to raise your awareness, so you may already know which thoughts you would like to change. In order to change your mind, you need to start creating new neuropathways. Just like the creation of any new path, it takes effort and work to begin with. Your neuropathways have to be built with new thoughts. Each new thought fires new neurons in your brain, and those neurons create the new path. So by choosing a new thought, you actually start to rewire your brain. I know, fucking amazing.

And, as if that's not exciting enough, the old neuropathways that you were used to following on a daily basis will get smaller and eventually disappear. Yes, your default way of thinking. Your current pathways will actually disappear.

Think of your neuropathways like plants. The plants that you repeatedly water every day will grow bigger, stronger, and take root. The pathways that don't get watered will wither away and die from lack of attention. It's your choice which plants you water.

Maybe you're someone who worries a lot. What if one of your consistent thoughts is "If my relationship doesn't work out, I'm going to end up lonely and alone." Yeah, it's sad, but no one worries about great shit happening, which is part of the problem, but I digress.

Every time you allow yourself to think that thought, you are strengthening the roots of that neuropathway. You are literally choosing to make it stronger. And the stronger it is, the more automatically you think it.

Now, let's say that one day you wake up and decide that you don't want to have those thoughts of worry anymore. They are not serving you, and in actual fact, you love your partner, and your relationship is great. You've realized that worrying is interfering with your happiness, and you know that your mind is malleable, so you can choose a new thought instead.

You can choose to think, "I love my partner and I love my life; all is well." It's so simple, yet when you choose to think and repeat this new thought, neurons fire together and you have created a new pathway. The more conscious you become, the more you will catch yourself if you divert to the old pathway, and you can quickly return to and repeat your chosen thought.

Yes, I am telling you that you can choose different thoughts and change the way your brain is wired.

What happens when you think the new thought over and over again? Exactly, you're so smart; it strengthens that neuropathway. What happens to the old worrisome thought that you are not choosing to think anymore? Yup, right again, you brilliant human! It shrinks, dies, and disappears, buh-bye!

Changing Your Default

Now that you know how you change your mind, it's important to realize that new neuropathways aren't created overnight. Your default thinking, which is the way you think when you're not being fully aware, will always take the strongest, most familiar pathway. The only way to create a strong pathway is to repeatedly think the same thought over and over and over and over.

So, this sounds awesome, right? But why does this matter? Well, it matters because your thoughts really do create your reality. It's not simply another platitude; it's the truth. Scientific and universal truth.

Allow me to elaborate.

You think a thought. That thought produces hormone stimulation in your brain. The hormones create and release chemicals. Those chemicals are your feelings. Your feelings inform your actions and behavior. Your actions and behavior create your results. Your results are your reality.

So, Thoughts = Feelings = Behavior = Results.

It's a loop. The "Everything starts with a thought" loop.

For all my visual peeps, check this out:

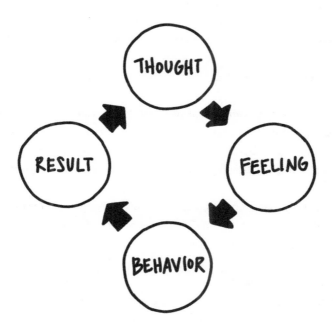

As soon as you choose to direct the "Everything starts with a thought" loop by inputting thoughts that serve you, you can change the default settings on your human technology. Powerful, or what?

Danielle was desperate to grow her coaching business. She claimed that she wasn't making enough money and that she was struggling to get clients, so we started working together to turn her business around.

"Tell me what action you're taking to build your business," I asked, so that we had a baseline from which to build upon.

"I go to networking groups, but no one talks to me; I never get any leads from the events I go to. I hate writing, so I'm not emailing potential clients because I'm sure my words will put them off, and I'm not doing any webinars or videos because it's too scary. I do mention my work to people when I can, but nobody seems interested."

"Okay, let's start with networking," I suggested, as I knew that once she understood the "Everything starts with a thought" loop, she could choose to work differently. "Tell me what you think about networking events and how you feel when you walk into an event."

"The groups are stupid, they're full of people trying to sell their own stuff, but I go because I should. When I walk in, I feel indifferent and 'meh.' I don't want to be there."

"Okay, so when you're there, do you try to engage one-to-one? Do you introduce yourself with passion, and do you follow up with the contacts you make?" I asked, knowing the answer.

Danielle smiled, shaking her head. "Um, no. No, I don't do those things."

"It's okay, you're actually proving yourself right, and as humans, we always want to prove ourselves right."

"What?" Danielle was genuinely confused. "Did you just tell me I was getting it right or wrong?"

"Your original thought is that networking events are stupid, and you only go along because you feel you should," I repeated. "You feel indifferent when you get there, which makes sense, because you think it's a stupid event, so you behave as if you're indifferent. You don't introduce yourself with passion, and you don't follow up on connections. It's no wonder that the result is zero leads. It's a loop. Your feelings and behaviors are determined by that first thought, which leads to a shitty result, proving that networking events are stupid."

Visual of Danielle's original thought loop:

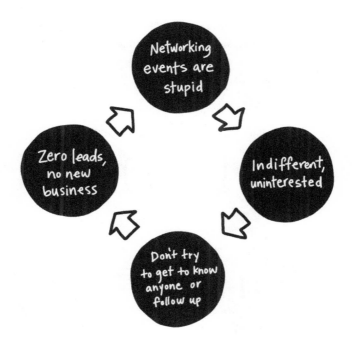

Danielle didn't know whether to be pleased or disappointed with herself. After all, humans do love to be right.

"Here's how we change your result," I continued. "You need to change that first thought. Before you go into a networking event, try repeating this new thought: 'I love what I do. I love sharing it with the world, and I can't wait to meet new people to share it with.' How does that feel?"

"Exciting and true; I do love what I do," she said, her eyes lighting up as she spoke her truth.

The following day, Danielle went to an event. She repeated the new thought all the way there. She was passionate, enthusiastic, and proudly looked people in the eye as she discussed her work. She followed up with every person she connected with, and guess what? By the end of the day, she had a new potential client meeting set up.

Visual of Danielle's new thought loop:

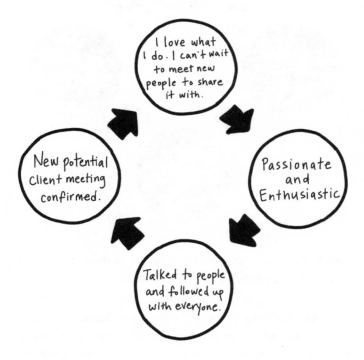

Amazing, right? This is what it means to change your thoughts, change your life.

Your thoughts are the starting point for absolutely everything. They kick-start every single area of your life—your business, your relationships, your parenting, your friendships, your money, your inner peace... all of it.

Recently married after a whirlwind romance, Debbie was head over heels in love. In the midst of the whirlwind, she hadn't had a chance to get to know her in-laws.

"Honestly, if I'd met them before the wedding, I'm not sure I'd be married now. They are so overbearing, I can't take it. Nobody in their family stands up to them. They are nosy, opinionated, and narrow-minded. I'm at my wit's end, and now they're coming for Thanksgiving and staying for a week. A WEEK. I would be stocking up on the pinot grigio, but I know they'll judge me for drinking."

"We need to look at this a different way if you're going to get through Thanksgiving unscathed," I said. "You sound angry as you're talking about them, and they're not even in the room, which shows you how powerful your thoughts are. Tell me how you feel when you're in a room with your in-laws."

"Frustrated, mainly. I feel excluded, and I'm afraid to challenge them on any of their views because I don't want to cause a scene. I don't have a relationship with them at all."

"Okay, so when you're feeling this way, how do you behave?" I prompted.

"I engage as little as possible. I sit in the corner of the room, drinking my pinot, counting down the seconds until I can escape to bed."

Visual of Debbie's original thought loop:

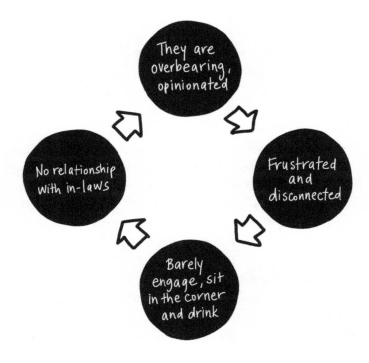

"That's no way to live!"

I could feel her despondence but was confident she could turn things around for Thanksgiving. "If this carries on, the relationship with your in-laws won't improve because it's difficult to engage when you feel that way, and it's difficult for anyone else to engage with someone who retreats to the corner of the room."

Debbie looked up when I said that. "What would you like your relationship with them to look like?"

"I'd love to have a relationship with them, to be a part of the family and be able to relax around them. It would definitely help my marriage if that could happen; I just don't know how to make it happen."

"How about if you come from a place of compassion and curiosity?" I asked. "If you take away the anger and frustration, you could say, 'These people are my family now, and I'm grateful they created such an amazing person together. I don't know what has happened in their lives to make them this way, but I'm open to learning.' How does that feel?"

"Okay, I could try that. And I really am grateful that they made such an amazing person!" That was the first time I had seen Debbie smile.

The week of the Thanksgiving visit flew by. Debbie repeated her new thoughts over and over again: "These people are my family. I'm so grateful they created such an amazing son. I don't know what their lives have been like, and I want to learn about them." Her new thoughts created a feeling of openness and curiosity.

Her in-laws still said some things that didn't align with her values, but she chose to engage without judgment and to connect and learn. It turned out that her in-laws also loved a glass of pinot, and they stayed up drinking, laughing, and getting to know each other.

Visual of Debbie's new thought loop:

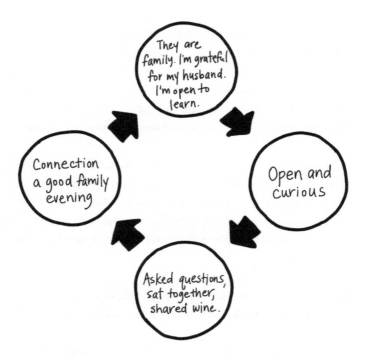

Debbie created a completely different outcome because she changed her thoughts. She ditched all expectations; she didn't expect her in-laws to change, so she took a different approach and created a new pathway, which led to the destination she had hoped to reach.

I know that you might be thinking, "Yeah, I get it, but it's not that easy to change your thoughts," and you're right, and wrong. Here's the thing: thoughts are just thoughts. Just because you think it doesn't make it real, doesn't make it true, and doesn't mean you have to believe it.

Let's say that again. Just because you think it doesn't make it real, doesn't make it true, and doesn't mean you have to believe it.

The ability to change your thoughts is what makes your mind the greatest tool you'll ever have. It is a tool. Plain and simple. Learn how to use it, and you will always be able to choose how you feel and direct yourself to achieve the results you want.

You have approximately sixty thousand thoughts per day. Per day! Of those sixty thousand thoughts, 95 percent of them are repetitive, which means you think the same thoughts over and over, every day. Wouldn't you like to have more authority over what's being repeated in your mind every day? That's why it is more important than ever to learn how to think on purpose.

How incredible would it be to be in control of how you feel? Exactly. Amazing.

"That's great, Tracy; these people have worked with you, so they had your help. But what about when I get cut off in traffic, or when my husband comes home late and doesn't call first, or when my boss passes me up for a promotion, or when a prospective client doesn't hire me? How can I feel happy when my circumstances aren't good?" Yup, I hear you!

This is where your inner power starts to take shape. I promise that you have this in you. It's up to you to choose to activate and use the information you're reading.

The Imprisoned and Empowered Mind

Here's the difference between an imprisoned mind and an empowered mind. It's the best way to show you that you have the power to transform your thinking by dropping in "choice."

Imprisoned Mind

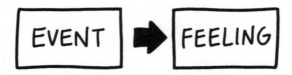

In the imprisoned mind model, you have the event, the thing that happened. When that thing happens, you automatically shoot directly into the feeling via the strongest neuropathway.

Empowered Mind

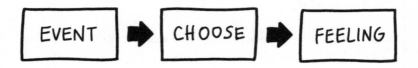

In the empowered mind model, you still have the event and you still shoot into a feeling, but there's a conscious decision to be made in between. You get to choose the thought and the meaning of the event. That middle box is where your inner power lives.

As you now know, when you change your thought, you change your feeling. BOOM!

When you are operating with an imprisoned mind and someone cuts you off in traffic, you are instantly pissed. The event takes you straight into the feeling.

When you are operating with an empowered mind and someone cuts you off in traffic, you choose. You choose to think, "I hope everything's okay; maybe there's a family emergency, so they have to rush," which takes you straight into feeling fine, calm, and at ease.

Choose the Meaning

Before thought comes meaning.

Here's the truth: everything is inherently meaningless. When you take a moment to think about this, you'll see that NOTHING means ANYTHING until you make it mean something, until you CHOOSE to infuse meaning into it.

Still with me? Good.

Nicole has been working for the same company for years. She is ready for a promotion. She has ticked every box, been a loyal employee, and dedicated way too many evenings and weekends to the company for this opportunity to pass her by. The application process is a formality, surely? Leaving the interview with a smile, she was confident that she'd get the job.

"What the actual fuck?" Nicole screamed on the phone to her best friend. "How could they give the job to someone else? What a kick in the teeth. That's it, I'm leaving, I hate corporate America. If they don't think I'm good enough, then I can't stay here."

At no point has anyone said that Nicole isn't good enough. That's the meaning she has attached to the circumstances.

She could attach any number of meanings. The extra responsibility would mean even more hours, and she wouldn't have time to start the book she has been desperate to write. The person who got the job had a new perspective, which will be a great way for her to learn another approach, as she's been working the same way for years. There's a better job, with the potential to earn more money, about to be advertised at a company closer to her home, and thankfully, she's now free to apply for it. Do you see how easy it is?

Jill's partner was late getting home, dinner was ruined, and there wasn't even a hint of an apology. The tornado of anger is rising. "You didn't even think to call to tell me you were going to be late. That tells me everything I need to know about how much you respect me."

It doesn't tell her that at all, does it? The meaning Jill has attached to the lack of communication is that it is disrespectful, but at this point, she has no idea what has happened to make her partner late. It could be anything from a personal disaster to the fact there was a lost cell phone and a late train. It's the automatic attachment of a meaning that has caused the feeling of anger, nothing else.

Infused meanings are not truth. Let's say that again: *infused meanings are not truth.*

Jenny is a divorced mother of two. She spends every day hoping that the relationship with her ex-husband improves, for the sake of their children, but it seems to be getting worse, and she doesn't know what to do about it.

She knew she needed to text him and nervously pressed *Send*. He was always attached to his phone, so she knew he'd read the message immediately. "Hey, the kids have a dentist appointment on Tuesday afternoon, and I might not be able to take them, could you?"

Twenty-four hours later, still no reply.

"He's just doing this to wind me up. He knows it drives me insane when I'm trying to plan my work schedule and he refuses to help. I bet he's laughing at me, waiting for me to text and ask again just so he can point out how impatient I am. How dare he just ignore me? It's no wonder I divorced the asshole. Oh, NOW he calls me."

Picking up the phone, Jenny was raring to go. "You know what? You can take your call and shove it. I needed a reply yesterday, and I've been forced to rearrange my whole week thanks to your incompetence as a father. Don't think for a second that I'm going to switch weekends now. If you can't be there for the children when they need you, don't bother being there at all."

"Jenny, I was calling to say I dropped my phone down the toilet yesterday. I raced into town on my lunch break to get a replacement and am calling to say, if it's not too late, of course I can take the children to the dentist."

"Oh."

No hidden meaning, no agenda, just a phone in a toilet.

Seriously, it's your thoughts that hold the power. And your meanings underpin your thoughts.

The Rabbit Hole of Hell

Being able to use your mind as the tool that it is means that you need to be hypervigilant about your meaning-making machine. Without awareness and monitoring, it is creating uninvited meanings all day long. If you're unaware of what's happening, it's more than likely that you will create meanings that are disempowering.

- I didn't get invited to that event; it must mean they don't like me.
- My daughter got a bad grade on her recent exam; it must mean she's going to fail her finals.
- I was laid off; it must mean I wasn't good enough.
- My lunch meeting is running late; it must mean they don't respect my time.
- The guy I went on a date with never asked me out again; it must mean something is wrong with me.

It's the rabbit hole of hell. You see, as soon as you attach a meaning to something and it becomes a thought, your brain automatically finds other thoughts that will prove you right. Then, before you know it, you're descending down the rabbit hole of hell.

Let's take this example. "My daughter got a bad grade on her recent exam; it must mean she's going to fail her finals." The rabbit hole looks like this: "She's really bad at taking tests. What if she fails her SATs? I knew she would fail. She has never been confident taking tests. I should have brought in a tutor to help her. OMG, what if she doesn't get into college. What is she going to do with her life? What if I have to support her forever? I feel sick. I need to lie down." DO YOU SEE THIS?

Let's do one more to make sure you're picking up what I'm putting down.

"My lunch meeting is running late; it must mean they don't respect my time." The rabbit hole looks like this: "My boss doesn't respect me. I hate when people don't respect my time. Why can't people just stick to the allocated time? It's so rude and disrespectful. Speaking of disrespect, I haven't heard from my husband all day; he's such an ass."

You're laughing because you know it's true.

Your mind does what it thinks you want it to do. So as soon as you infuse a meaning, that meaning becomes the driving thought. Then your mind takes that driving thought as a directive and runs with it! We're looking for examples or other thoughts that make us feel disrespected, got it. And down the rabbit hole of hell you go.

Choosing your meanings and thoughts are nonnegotiable if you want something different than you currently have. If you want to get out of the rabbit hole.

Fortunately, because inherently everything is meaningless, you have some options. You can simply choose to live in the meaninglessness of it all. Otherwise known as IS-NESS. Simply stating it IS. It is not good or bad, empowering or disempowering—it just is.

Introducing Is-Ness

Everything is inherently neutral, devoid of meaning. It simply is. Remember that popular cliché—it is what it is—well, that's what we're talking about.

IS-ness is inherent meaninglessness.

You can choose to create and infuse a meaning that is empowering in any given situation, or you can choose a meaning that feels disempowering. If you're looking for freedom and inner peace, I strongly recommend that you practice meaninglessness. Choose to remain neutral. Choose to live in IS-NESS.

All you have to do to practice meaninglessness is release the habit of infusing any meaning at all.

Consider these:

- If it rains, we don't question the reason why. Rain is something that happens; it's what the sky and clouds do sometimes.
- When we see birds flying, we don't say, "Why the fuck is the bird flying? Is it trying to get away from me?" Of course we don't. We accept that birds fly.
- We love to see flowers growing, and we don't question why they're growing. It's what they do: they grow. We accept that and don't give it a second thought.

Here's a meaning(less)-making visual for you. I dropped in some examples for you to check out.

Try it and find out for yourself how easy it is to shift the meanings that you create.

Now, drop the circumstances or events you're dealing with in the middle column.

The *truth* is and always will be that whatever that circumstance is, it's meaningless.

You can then see how you can choose to infuse disempowering or empowering meaning.

DISEMPOWERING	IS-NESS	EMPOWERING
So disrespectful. I'm so annoyed!	Lunch meeting ran late.	More time for myself to listen to that podcast.
She's going to fail the semester. Oh god.	Daughter got a bad grade on exam.	No biggie, she'll learn from it and do better next time
What if I'm not as good as I thought? My business isn't going well.	Potential client didn't hire me.	I know she'll find the right fit. There's many more ideal clients coming my way.
There's something wrong with me. I'll never find the one.	Guy I went on a date with never called back.	His loss! I'm amazing.

—   Neutral   +

Everything can be neutral because, in actual fact, everything is neutral. The truth is that nothing means anything until you make it mean something.

Want to feel light, at ease, and be totally untouchable by your external circumstances? Choose IS-NESS.

Energetic Thinking

There are two universal laws that prove to us that our thoughts create our reality.

1. We are all made up of energy.
2. Like energy attracts like energy.

Do you remember that as a human being, you are made of atoms, molecules, and cells? Of course you do because you are so smart! Well, when you dig a little deeper into the inner workings of atoms, molecules, and cells, you find that there is nothing there, nothing tangible, anyway. You find energy, just waves of energy vibrating at a specific frequency.

YOU ARE ENERGY.

If you want to change your life, then it's time to start thinking on purpose. When you are feeling higher-level feelings, you are simultaneously raising your energy. This is because higher-level feelings vibrate at a higher frequency.

Your thoughts carry energy. Your energy is a frequency, a vibration, and it's that vibration that determines how you show up in the world. If you're thinking low-level thoughts, you'll be operating at a low-level frequency. If you're thinking high-level thoughts, you'll be operating at a high-level frequency.

Your frequency attracts more of the same to you.

If you are feeling frustrated, negative, angry, disappointed, and stressed, then you will attract more of the same into your life.

If you are feeling happy, joyful, and optimistic, then you will attract more of the same into your life.

It's your choice.

Sweet FA (Focus and Attention)

We cannot have a conversation about the power of your mind without talking about the power of your focus and attention. I call it the Power of FA, and it's another element of mind mastery that you have at your disposal.

I'm talking about what you choose to focus on and where you choose to place your attention, day in and day out. Where your attention goes, your energy flows.

Up until now you might not have realized that what you focus on and why you're focusing on it is so critical. The truth is, it is central to creating the life you desire.

If you place your focus and attention on the future, then you are placing yourself into the unknown, which will induce anxiety and worry. If you place your focus and attention on the past, then you are placing yourself into that which you cannot change, which will induce rumination and depression.

Where you place your attention is where you place your energy. The more attention you place on something, the more of it you'll get in your life. If you put your FA on how stressed out you are, the latest argument with your spouse, or the money you haven't made yet, then you are choosing to receive more and more of the same. Did you get that? More and more of the same. Is that what you want?

This is science, so you can hold your skepticism. This shit is REAL.

"Tracy, I can't deal with this anymore. It's too much."

That's always a good start to a call. My client, Marie, was on the edge.

"My daughter's attitude is destroying our family, my husband and I are fighting about how to deal with her, and no matter what I do, her behavior isn't getting any better—it's getting worse."

"So, you're focusing on the problem. Let's see how we can shift things," I started to say.

"What else is there to focus on? Honestly, she's turning into someone I don't recognize, and her behavior is disgraceful. This is not how we raised her. It's such a difficult situation. I feel guilty all the time; I must have done something wrong as a parent. My already short fuse is getting shorter by the day, and the continual arguments make our home a living nightmare."

"Tell me something positive your daughter did this morning," I asked, sure that there must have been something.

"Something positive?" Marie laughed. "Are you joking?"

"Think about this morning. Tell me one thing that your daughter did that was positive." I wasn't letting this go.

"I guess she did help out with her brother. She helped him tie his shoelaces before we left for school, but then she spilled juice on the kitchen table and refused to clean it up."

"Okay, so she helped? That was kind of her. Did you thank her for helping?"

"Well, no, I was too busy trying to clean up the mess she had made."

In that moment, Marie started to soften and could see what she was doing. She was so busy focusing her attention on the behaviors that she found problematic that she was missing out on the positive things her daughter did.

"You will always see what you look for. That's how it works. So if you are focusing on the frustration, on the problem, you will only see more of that, making the situation worse and worse," I explained. "You're waking up into the anticipation of another terrible, frustrating morning. You're stressed and on edge before anything even takes place. That energy is palpable and impacts everyone. Without intention, you are waiting to experience her 'terrible behavior,' and so that is what gets created. What would it feel like to shift and focus on your daughter's positives? What if you woke up light and happy, played some music and anticipated a happy, fun morning?"

"Sounds amazing. I feel better just thinking about it," Marie said.

Marie did just that. I remember the sound in her voice a few days later.

"It's magic. It feels like magic. It's amazing how much better our mornings are. So much more love and peace."

That shift in focus and attention allowed Marie to notice all of the positive behaviors her daughter displayed on a daily basis. It allowed her to shift the energy of her household. It allowed her to feel more connected with her whole family. And since this goodness was the new place of her focus and attention, she got more and more of it.

What you look for, you will see. It's ridiculously simple, and it all comes down to your Reticular Activating System (RAS). The part of your brain that shows you what you look for.

The input from four of your five senses are wired directly into your RAS (your sense of smell is wired to connect to the emotional center of your brain, so for the sake of this RAS conversation, it doesn't apply). The RAS is a filter for your mind, making sure you don't have to deal with more information than you can handle. As you can imagine, it has its work cut out for it in the modern world. It plays a huge role in what you perceive to be true. It decides what is important for you to see and is the gatekeeper of the information that is received by your conscious mind. Your RAS is like the bouncer at a nightclub.

So, how does it know what's important to us? How does it know what we want to see?

It's automatic. The first filter is all about safety and keeping you alive, but beyond that we are directing our RAS through the programming in our subconscious mind, the thoughts you think, and where you place your FA. This is why choosing where you place your focus and attention is critical. Your RAS can only look for what your thoughts are telling it to look for.

It doesn't care what you're asking for; it doesn't distinguish between what's true or helpful to you. It simply delivers based on your thoughts. If you feel angry, it will find you more to feel angry about. If you feel overwhelmed, it will find you more to feel overwhelmed about. If you are worried, it will find more for you to worry about. You get the picture.

It works on a practical level too. Let's say you decide that you want a new car, and you deserve one, you worthy human you! You decide you want to get a white Jeep. Over the course of a few weeks, you test drive a few, you go online and price them out, and you get a subscription to *Jeep* magazine. You're going all in. Then, what feels like "all of a sudden," you start seeing them everywhere. Everywhere you drive, you see white Jeeps. You're freaking out! You call your best friend and say, "You're never gonna believe this. I have just seen six white Jeeps in one day; it must be a sign. It must mean that the universe wants me to get the Jeep!"

Um, no, it doesn't, but congratulations on confirming you have a fantastically functioning RAS. It is not a universal sign that you're supposed to get a white Jeep. It's a consequence of the shift in your focus and attention.

Where you place your FA is woven into your story, and your story is woven into your FA.

We all have stories. They're basically a collection of our beliefs and thoughts strung together. We live in our stories, and they become our truth even though they're not necessarily true. I'm talking about big, overarching lifetime stories like:

- I had a really rough childhood, and everything is hard for me.
- My brother was the smart one; I'm not good enough. Success won't happen for me.
- Emotion is weakness; I'm strong and get shit done without needing to ask for help. I'm fine.
- No one has ever really liked me. I'm not pretty enough. I'll never find someone to marry me.

Along with our lifetime stories, we create chapters that are relevant to what's going on in our lives at any given time.

- My boss has it in for me.
- My kid is making the household crazy.
- If I start my dream business, everyone will judge me. Who am I to run my own business?
- My husband cheated on me because I wasn't good enough. My divorce is my fault, and my life is over.

You will always live up to your story because it is what you believe to be true. It's where you're placing your FA, so it's all you can see.

I understand if you're feeling resistance to this. The thing is that what I'm teaching you is not optional. It's how your brain works, how science works, how the universe works. It's fact.

The great news about stories is that you can tell a new one anytime you like. You can rewrite your stories to support the life you actually want to be living, one that supports your limitlessness, your power, your awesomeness.

Shifting Your Focus and Attention

It's time to make the choice to shift your focus and attention. Use your increased awareness to start paying attention to where you put your attention!

THE WORK

- Set an alarm on your phone to go off a few times a day with the questions: What am I focusing on right now? Where am I placing my attention?
- You will be shocked to discover what your mind was focusing on. Honestly, our minds should never be left unattended.
- You can play a game with your RAS so you can experience the power of this. Pick a color, any color. Think about that color and pay attention to your surroundings for the next forty-eight hours. You'll be surprised by all the things around you in that color that you never noticed before. Go on, try it.

Talking Mind and Body

I am compelled to take a brief moment and acknowledge something critical about your mind and body. Your mind and body talk to each other all day long. Your mind and your body are connected. You may be thinking, "Well, obviously." But no, not really so obvious, because so many of us don't truly live life with this awareness.

If you walk around wearing stress and overwhelm like badges

of honor, thinking disempowering thoughts, then you are likely fatigued, burnt-out. You're not a victim of your life or a victim of yourself. You're not forced to live in stress, negativity, and overwhelm. No one is making you go so fast and hustle so hard that you take no time for yourself.

What can all of this shit create? You guessed it: physical ailments like headaches, migraines, back pain, and tension in your body. It's *dis-ease*. It's because your mind is creating your inner environment and your inner environment exists in your body.

It is more important than ever to master your mind, so you can actually experience your life in a way that serves you, the way you deeply desire and the way you absolutely, indisputably deserve.

It's always made me laugh that we don't really appreciate that the mind and body are connected. We are one being, and we need to stop treating our mind and body as separate entities.

Your brain is connected to your brain stem, which is connected to your spine, which runs through your body. Any thought that you allow to go past your conscious awareness passes right through your brain stem, right down into your body. See, incontestable connection.

MIND-SET

All of this contributes to why mindset is a word that we hear regularly now. It's a word that is going to change the world. And already has.

Your mindset is what you think and believe about any given thing or situation.

See it like this: MIND-SET. Whatever your mind is "set" to is exactly what will be. You will never outperform what your mind is set to, regardless of how desperately you want to. In fact, that desperation puts it even further out of reach.

Think about the governor on the engine of your car. Have you noticed that your speedometer says your car goes up to 200 mph, but when you floor it, it doesn't actually go past 160 mph? Okay, most of us haven't actually tried to max out the speed of our cars, but the point of my story remains true. There is a governor on the engine that limits and prohibits the car. It is not able to go any faster than what the governor is SET to. It doesn't matter how hard you press on the gas or how much you want, hope, and wish for extra speed. It won't happen.

It's the same for you. In truth you are a limitless being. Seriously, you are unstoppable and possess endless potential. But you have mind-sets about yourself and areas of your life that limit your ability to progress. Until you change your mindset, you won't change your life.

Which means using your mind as the greatest and most incredible tool you'll ever have access to *is* the gateway to everything.

Mastering the Invisible

The first important thing that I think we can all agree on is that you can't see your thoughts. They're invisible.

In order to master your invisible thoughts, your mind magic, you need to become aware of your feelings. Your feelings are the guidance system that shows you what you're thinking.

If you are feeling stressed, you are thinking stressed-out thoughts. If you are feeling low and shitty, you are thinking low and shitty thoughts. If you are feeling insecure, you are thinking thoughts of insecurity.

THE WORK

Practice these two mindset tools, and
you will master the invisible.

- Don't Believe Everything You Think:
  - Become aware that you are not feeling the way you want to feel.
  - Choose to pause, take a deep breath, and go up into your mind. Find the thought or statement that is creating the feeling.
  - Write the thought down on paper.
  - Observe the thought that you are now seeing on the paper. Read it out loud.
  - Now you can clearly see that you are NOT your thought. The thought is no longer even a part of you. Since you are the thing reading the thought outside you, you are now observing the thought. Therefore, the thought is not you.
  - Now it's time question that thought. Questioning is an essential part of this process as you grow the skill of thinking on purpose.
    - Who am I when I attach to this thought?
    - How do I act when I think this thought?
    - Does this thought bring me peace or stress?
    - What is believing this thought costing me?
    - How is this thought serving me?
    - Can I see a reason to drop the thought?
    - Who am I without this thought? (This questioning

> process is inspired by and based on the work of Byron
> Katie, the pioneer of questioning your thoughts.)
> - Now, you can make a CHOICE. Keep the thought or trash the
>   thought. If you choose to keep it, you literally have to put it back
>   into your mind and actively repeat it. That doesn't sound like the
>   best use of your time.
>
> This is an extremely powerful process that will change your life if
> you do the work. Start choosing the thoughts that serve you, and
> don't believe everything you think.
>
> - Feed Your Mind—The Side by Side:
>   - Grab a piece of paper and draw a line down the center.
>   - On the top left, write "My Mind Says." On the top right,
>   write "But I Say."
>   - Allow yourself to throw up all the shit your mind is offering
>   you on the left. Get it all out. Then take a deep breath and
>   shake your body out.
>   - Then go over to the right side. This is where you think on
>   purpose. This is where you choose the thoughts that align
>   with how you want to feel, what you want to do, and who
>   you want to be in that moment. Your new neuropathways,
>   if you will.
>
> You'll notice that the sides actually feel like two different people.
> The more you do this practice, the more you will embrace and see
> that you are not your mind. You are the director of it.

Repeat our **Worthy Human Mantra** after me:

I am worthy. I am enough. I am powerful. I get to choose.

Choice #5
ARE YOU READY TO GIVE UP THE SHIT THAT IS *Killing* YOUR SOUL?

When I decided to write this book, I knew that to serve you in the most powerful way possible, I needed to address what I call the Life Suckers.

The Life Suckers are behaviors and habits that suck your energy, take from you, and keep you away from the profound happiness, joy, and success that you deserve.

The bad news is they're only with you because you have chosen them, but the good news is you can delete these Life Suckers whenever you want to. Now that you're well versed in Radical Personal Responsibility, you know exactly what to do.

Strap yourself in and hold onto the safety rails as we begin this ride. We are going to hang out and identify the Life Suckers one by one. You can then choose to rid yourself of them, and as you do, you will instantly raise your frequency, get closer to your authentic self, and increase your happiness.

Life Sucker Number One—Control

"I've learned that when you try and control everything, you enjoy nothing."
—UNKNOWN

For my proud control freaks out there, it might feel like I'm asking you to leave your happy place when I ask you to release your need to control everything. Trust me: I promise, you'll be fine. You'll be better than fine.

According to *Webster's Dictionary*, control is defined as "the power to direct people's behavior or the course of events." Seriously, I had never looked up the definition until I wrote this book. Holy shit, even the definition is exhausting. Direct people's behavior or the course of events? Um, I'm sorry, are you Mary Poppins? That sounds like an enormous amount of stress and responsibility to me.

Our conversation is not about other people. Our conversation is about how YOUR need to control is impacting and limiting YOU.

When you are controlling, you have a need for everything to go the way you want it to go.

When you think you can control everything, or feel the need to control everything, the amount of stress, tension, and anxiety that you experience is more than I can articulate.

As a recovering control freak myself, I am well versed in this arena. I remember the moment I surrendered control. It was when I became a single mother. As a co-parent, I share custody of my daughter, so for 50 percent of the time she wasn't with me. For a long while I attempted to control what my daughter was doing, where she was, and what was happening when she wasn't with me.

She was awake super late one night, way past her bedtime according to my rules. The rules were different at her dad's house, and I didn't like that. His parenting style gave her so much more freedom than mine did, and I didn't like that either. Neither one of us was wrong nor right, we just had different parenting styles. But as a control freak, this drove me batshit crazy.

The problem wasn't the co-parenting. The problem was my need to attempt to control what was happening when my daughter wasn't with me. Side note: the problem is never the problem. The problem is our thinking about the circumstance or situation.

I was choosing to attempt to control something that didn't need any input from me at all.

I use the word "attempt" intentionally because you never actually have control over anything. Ever.

The only thing I actually accomplished was driving myself crazy. I created feelings of anger and frustration, and I was nowhere near as happy as I could have been if I had simply surrendered.

Feeling all of that anger, frustration, and tension taught me that I didn't want to feel that way. At all. Like, ever.

It was a powerful lesson, and through my own reflection, I made a decision that I am eternally grateful for. I chose to let it go. My level of peace and ease around my co-parenting relationship is now awe-inspiring.

Control is the opposite of peace and ease. When you are controlling, you are constricted. You are creating tension and pressure.

THE WORK

Stop right now, take a deep breath, and connect to your body. Does it feel tight, tense, or constricted? Does it feel open, loose, and expanded? Exactly. That tightness is what control feels like. If pain and stiffness around your neck and shoulders feels familiar to you, that's control.

Everyone lands somewhere on the spectrum of control and for good reason. We were brought up in an environment of control. Bells rang to tell us when to move, with rules upon rules telling us what we could and couldn't do, and endless expectations from everyone around us.

To imagine a life without being in control feels scary because if you aren't in control, then what will happen? If you aren't controlling people and outcomes, then you are entering a world of the unknown and unfamiliar. Your brain hates unfamiliar. It will do anything it can to keep you in an environment that feels familiar, but the control thing is hurting you.

Think about it: you run yourself ragged trying to control everything. Your mind is consumed with the need for things to be a certain way. You are tense, highly strung, and sucked dry as a result. Quite frankly, I want more for you than that.

We're going to start practicing openness and allowance. This practice leads to the fabulous feelings of peace and ease. You can choose to let go of the need to control. You can choose to surrender.

When you surrender, you open yourself up to receive and to feel abundant. The irony is that when you stop controlling, you get more than you could have ever imagined.

Ready to become a recovering control freak?

THE WORK

Become aware of when you are feeling stress, tension, and constriction. Where do you feel the stress and tension in your body? Ask yourself, "What am I controlling or attempting to control right now?"

Recognize it; take a deep breath and surrender. The thing about surrender is there's no "how-to." It's a choice. You choose to surrender because you're ready to be at ease.

You can also practice the Serenity Prayer because you know how powerful it is to plant the seed of a new thought: "Grant me the serenity to accept the things I cannot change, the courage to change the things I can, and the wisdom to know the difference."

Life Sucker Number Two—Expectation

> *"Expectation is the root of all heartache."*
> — WILLIAM SHAKESPEARE

We cannot discuss control without also discussing its faithful partner, expectation.

By definition, an expectation is a strong belief that something **will happen or be a certain way**; a belief that someone **should** do, achieve, or act in a certain way. That "someone" includes YOU.

Expectations are toxic. Ninety-nine percent of the time they are the cause of your frustration and disappointment. Yup, it's true, and you will soon experience this shocking truth for yourself.

If you're thinking, "I don't have a lot of expectations," I am asking you, with love, to think again.

Your expectations are hidden everywhere: from huge life expectations to situational expectations, expectations of others to expectations of yourself.

- My mother wasn't supposed to die when I was young.
- My husband wasn't supposed to have an accident.
- I wasn't supposed to have breast cancer.
- I wasn't supposed to be a single mother.
- Life's not fair.
- This is not where I should be at this age.
- I shouldn't have lost my job.
- That wasn't supposed to happen to me.
- She shouldn't talk to me that way.
- Tonight's party is going to be perfect.

Somewhere along the line we started believing that life was supposed to look a certain way. We believe that we had a say. But we don't, and those things happened. Remember is-ness? Holding on to these expectations of life means that you're arguing with reality. That will always lead to suffering, disappointment, and at times, anxiety and depression. The power to let go of believing that life was supposed to look a certain way lies within you and only you.

When we walk around with tons of expectations about how things should be and then feel disappointed by the fact that they're not, we are creating our own feelings of disappointment. Are you getting this? It's huge. You can set yourself free! And yes, this is Radical Personal Responsibility and the power of choice.

If you're thinking, "But if I don't have expectations of what I want my daughter to do, or what I need my employee to deliver, or how I need my husband to help, then how does anything happen?" I totally hear you. I have a solution for you because I'm nice like that: you can choose to make an agreement.

Creating agreements is the mutually beneficial replacement for expectations. An agreement allows you to discuss what you want or need. It also allows the other person to express their wants and needs. Together, you have banished expectation.

It's quite magical.

Lauren started working with me because she was disappointed with every aspect of her life.

"My business isn't at the stage I had planned for it to be after five years of working nonstop. I'm disappointed in myself and my team that we haven't managed to achieve the goals we set. My partner is no help. Living together isn't the blissful existence I thought it would be, and I think we're on the verge of separating."

"Let's look at what's going on at work?" I asked, as bringing in more clients was one of the goals Lauren wanted to look at.

"The team has a series of actions for this quarter. We're already at the start of March, and they're nowhere near completing the lists I gave them."

"The lists you GAVE them?" I could see where this was going. Lauren worked as part of a collaborative team, or at least that's what she described it as when we first met.

"Well, yes. I need to make sure we achieve what we set out to achieve, and we all need to work harder. They should know that."

"Should they? Have you discussed it with them?"

She took a moment before steadfastly replying, "No, I shouldn't need to. Isn't it obvious?"

No sooner had the words left her mouth when she let out an exhausted sigh and whispered, "I'm expecting the impossible, aren't I? And I didn't even discuss it."

"Bingo," I replied.

Lauren called the team together to talk about why the business wasn't reaching its potential and how, as a team, they could work to change things. This wasn't a meeting where she was going to drop another list of deliverables or expectations. Clearly, she already knew where that approach got her. This was a meeting to create intentional agreements.

She shared her vision for the company. She shared the goals and priorities that she'd like them to achieve. Then she asked them for their feedback: "Knowing you are doing the work, where do you need more support to make this happen? What do you see as obstacles from where you sit? Based on what all of these goals require, are the timelines reasonable?"

The team was engaged and gave great, honest feedback. Through creating agreements, there was buy-in. The team felt heard, which inspired them and helped them feel vested.

Lauren realized how many innovative ideas her team had and how their new agreements on making the company vision a reality would undoubtedly transform the business. And it did. Not only did the revenue increase, but the employees got closer, and the company communication improved.

You can choose to ditch your expectations and choose to form agreements, relax, and let go. You will probably find yourself pleasantly surprised by what comes your way when you make this choice.

I remember when I started to become aware of my expectations. Damn, it hurt, and the list was long. I used to experience a ton of frustration around the way my daughter did her homework. I would walk into her room to check in with her, and she would be lying on her stomach, on the floor, with her laptop in front of her, papers strewn all over the place, with her headphones on, listening to music.

"What are you doing?" I asked as she reluctantly pressed pause.

"Homework."

I could feel my blood start to boil. "Homework? How can you possibly learn like that? You can't. Get up and sit at your desk. That's why you have a desk!"

She looked at me and calmly said, "Mom, I'm fine. I like to listen to music when I study. Leave me alone. It's fine."

I should have left it there, but I didn't. "It's not fine. This is not okay. You can't learn like that."

"Mom, everything is great. My grades are good, my teachers love me, everything's fine. Why are you making a problem where's there's no problem?"

I was speechless. Damn it! I was the problem. I took a deep breath and said, "You're right, carry on."

My controlling, expectation-led, life-sucking ways were the problem.

What my daughter said to me became the agreement. As long as she gives her best effort, her grades are good, and all is well, then she can study however, wherever, and whenever she wants. If something in those outcomes shifts, then it's time to have a conversation and make some changes.

THE WORK

Become an expectation detective.

- Pay attention when you feel disappointed, frustrated, or let down.
- When you notice the feeling, pause and ask yourself, "Where is

this coming from? Am I holding onto an expectation of myself, of someone else, of a situation, or of life in general? Am I arguing with reality?"
- When you have that insight, you get to choose.
- You can choose to simply realize you are creating your own frustration and disappointment, and release the expectation. Or you can create an agreement between you and the other side of the situation.

Life Sucker Number Three—Judgment

"When you judge another, you do not define them, you define yourself."
—WAYNE DYER

It's enough already. This one should have ended after high school. I know you're either thinking, "I'm not judgmental" or "It's so hard not to have an opinion." The truth is that it's NOT so hard to NOT have an opinion. It's just a default behavior. And it's so widely accepted by our society because so many people do it that it's easy to dismiss it or minimize how destructive and detrimental it is.

Judgment or being judgmental is a surefire way to increase your negativity and stress and keep you in a low-level state.

It's that continual unspoken—or spoken—reel of criticism and opinion that plays throughout your day.

- She can't afford that.
- He's so conceited posting all those selfies.

- She's so lazy.
- She's such a bitch.
- Why would anyone want to dress like that?
- He has no idea how to do his job.
- He's just trying to make money off of me.
- She is totally incompetent.
- Can you believe she left him after everything he went through?

This is resonating, isn't it? Your awareness is growing, and as you already know, awareness is everything.

So, where does judgment come from?

Our behavior of judgment stems from our need to protect ourselves. We judge when we don't align with someone else's ideals or beliefs. We judge when we feel insecure about ourselves. We judge when we feel left out.

When we judge, we are really longing for connection and acceptance, but in some totally ass-backwards way, instead of showing up vulnerable and open, we judge and shut down. It's self-preservation.

Another huge motivator for quitting judgment is the profound and instant impact it has on the judgment you feel you're receiving from others. Do you feel like you are always being judged? If so, start taking a look at all of your outgoing judgments, and you'll start to notice that they're a mirror.

Those who feel judged, judge others. Those who don't judge don't feel judged by others. Period.

How many more minutes and hours would you get back each day if you removed judgment from your to-do list? I know, probably a nauseating amount.

When you feel whole and fulfilled, judgment is not something you experience. When you love and accept yourself, judgment is not something you experience. When you are happy, judgment is not something you experience.

In addition, the other HUGE gift of giving up judgment is that you also effortlessly move closer to releasing comparison.

Why is that, you ask? Well, it's because judgment and comparison are married. If you are making comparisons, you are also making judgments. You can't have one without the other.

So, how do you start shifting this ugly, low-level behavior?

Yes, awareness. You know me so well.

Then what? With awareness about judgment comes curiosity. You cannot judge and be curious simultaneously. Seriously, your mind can't do both at the same time. Try it on.

Michelle had been told about the new guy, Aaron, who was going to be joining her team. He was an "old friend" of the boss, someone with a reputation of arrogance, and rumor had it he was a real kiss-up to anyone he deemed more superior than himself. She hadn't met him, but she already didn't like him.

"He's only been here a couple of weeks, and already I'm considering what I'll write in my letter of resignation. The boss has said he's not happy with the 'misalignment' between us, but I honestly can't work with the guy."

I hadn't seen Michelle this worried about work before, and to her credit, she was completely honest when I asked, "How are you acting toward him?"

"I don't like him. Let's say I'm not my best self," she admitted. "I can barely bring myself to say 'Good morning' to him, he's such a conceited asshole. I wait to respond to his emails; I'm so easily aggravated and triggered when we're in meetings together. It's like he says black and I say white. Ugh, he drives me crazy."

"Interesting. Have you actually spoken with him one-to-one since he started?"

"Of course, we've been in meetings together. We work in the same office. Well, no, actually, I haven't spoken to him directly. As in a real one-on-one conversation."

"So why do you believe he's such an asshole?"

"Sam from marketing and a few other people told me all about him, so when he joined the team, I already knew what he was like, and he's lived up to everything I've been told."

Michelle was living in quite a story. A story built off a thought of judgment based on low-level conversations and opinions from other people. She was experiencing a result of her own making.

In truth, she didn't know anything about him. She had no first-hand information, nor was she even able to give him a shot because she was so rooted in her thought of judgment.

Remember our "Everything starts with a thought" loop?

Consider the loop:

Thought of judgment–Aaron's an arrogant asshole who thinks he's better than everyone.

Feelings of–negativity, anger, disconnection.

Feelings influence behavior of–not engaging him, saying white when he says black, not being responsive.

Behavior creates the result of–a distant business relationship where they stay separate. Aaron responds to Michelle in kind.

Watch closely: the result allows Michelle to say, "See, I told you he was an arrogant asshole." That's why it's a loop. The result will always prove the original thought right.

You see it clearly now, don't you?

So, Michelle was tasked with getting curious. She did. She started with being curious in meetings and open to his suggestions. Then she chose to be curious and have a few direct conversations where she showed up open and reachable. And yes, you guessed it.

Not only are Michelle and Aaron great coworkers, but they are actually friends outside of the office.

When we judge, we leave little room for compassion and connection.

Now, I would like you to do the same thing. I'm tasking you with getting curious. I'm sure you can think of someone that you have made a judgment about, someone you feel disconnected from or less than pleasing feelings about when you think about them.

Through your curiosity, you can begin to find connection.

THE WORK

Pause here and self-assess. Who do you feel disconnected from? Where in your life can you sprinkle more curiosity? Is the judgment you have made based on truth or opinion?

Curiosity and wonder change everything. Inherently, curiosity connects while judgment separates.

Choose wisely.

Life Sucker Number Four—Comparison

"Comparison is an act of violence against oneself."
— IYANLA VANZANT

Want to know the fastest way to breed self-doubt, insecurity, and low self-esteem while igniting the flame on your "I'm not enough" campfire? Comparison. That's right: it does all that and more!

To compare means to measure or note the similarity or dissimilarity between yourself and someone else, personally or in circumstance. It's funny that the meaning mentions similarity because we never really use comparison to underscore how alike we are.

When we compare, we always default to comparing the dissimilarity, the difference, and always in the direction of driving ourselves to feel like shit.

We compare our most negative version of ourselves against the perceived "picture-perfect" version of someone else.

- **Comparison scenario one.** When you're exhausted and arguing with your partner at home, you jump on social media, and the first thing you see is a picture of your friend and her husband on vacation. Of course, you automatically start thinking that they have the perfect marriage, that she's so lucky, and the outcome of those thoughts is that you now feel like shit.

- **Comparison scenario two.** You're six months into your entrepreneurial journey, yet you start measuring yourself against someone who's been on their entrepreneurial journey for fifteen years. You're thinking that she's so successful, that everything she does is awesome and effortless. The next thought is that you're acutely aware that you're not at that stage and you wish you were. The outcome of those thoughts is that you now feel like shit.
- **Comparison scenario three.** You've been questioning your purpose and feeling lost in your job. Just as you start to wonder if life will ever go your way, your friend calls to tell you that she's moving to California to accept an awesome new job. Sure, you say congratulations, but then your thoughts start wondering why everything is working out so perfectly for her. You know that you've been working super hard for years and nothing like this has happened for you. It's not fair. The outcome of those thoughts is that you now feel like shit.

You feel like shit because you made the choice to follow the path of comparison. Your choice. Your choice. Your choice. Yes, I know I said that three times.

Oh, and another thing about this slippery slope of comparison: none of the shit you are making up in your head is true.

Behind that vacation photo, the truth is they went on that vacation in an attempt to save their marriage. It didn't work, and when they get home, they are officially separating.

While you're looking at the leading experts in your field, you can choose to think, "I've been an entrepreneur for six months; she's been doing it for fifteen years. What an inspiration! I will make sure my journey is just as successful."

While you are immersed in comparison with your friend, you don't remember the endless extra hours she has been working to be in a position to be offered this job in Cali. It was a tough decision as she is leaving her friends and family behind, but she's putting a positive spin on it.

When we are in comparison, we are making shit up. The truth is we know nothing. We know nothing about what is or isn't going on in the lives of other people. Continuing to compare yourself is taking you further and further away from your dreams, from a place of empowerment, and from a place of happiness.

When you are in comparison, you are in someone else's business. When you are in someone else's business, you are ignoring your own. So mind your own business. Stay focused on you.

There is one thing you need to do in order to choose to leave comparison behind for good. Come in closely: you have to choose to stay in your own lane.

Imagine two lanes side by side. Picture yourself in your lane, doing your thing and having a great time. You look over, check out the lane next to you, and decide that everything in that lane is infinitely better than in your lane. So, you jump out of your lane and into theirs.

Picture it: you're in *their* lane, getting into *their* business.

If you're in their lane with them, who's in your lane? Ding ding, that's right. NOBODY. Nobody is in your lane moving your life and dreams forward.

STAY IN YOUR LANE

THE WORK

Whenever you are tempted to compare yourself to someone else, repeat the words "STAY IN MY LANE" until the feeling passes.

Life Sucker Number Five—
Caring about What Other People Think

"Your life isn't yours if you constantly
care about what others think."
— ANONYMOUS

This one is HUGE. Being oblivious to what other people think is a game changer.

We place so much of our value on outside approval. Have you found yourself thinking any of these thoughts?

- Oh my God. What are "they" going to think?
- What if "they" don't like it?
- What if "they" don't like me?
- If I say how I really feel, "they" won't invite me.
- I can't say no; what would "they" think?

I'm fucking exhausted just typing it. Don't worry; you're not alone in thinking these thoughts. Please remember that you are worthy, you are enough, and you deserve to create a life where the only opinion that matters is your own. You can be your own validation.

Where does this totally irrational and unproductive obsession about what other people think come from?

To really get this, we have to travel back in time. We're going back tens of thousands of years to tribal times. Being part of your tribe was essential to survival. If you were rejected by your tribe, it could lead to your death. Being part of a tribe provided protection and food, everything you needed to stay alive. Being approved of, accepted, and liked actually meant you could continue living and breathing. Being accepted was a big deal back in tribal times.

Even though we have evolved and progressed quite a bit, this part of our evolutionary history has resulted in an unhealthy, disempowering obsession with what people think of us. It's as if our lives depend on it, but they don't, not anymore. In fact, it's quite the opposite.

Now you know that you can challenge that incessant need you have to be accepted. You have the power to choose a different path. Understanding is power.

You no longer live in a world where you need to rely on others for survival. This behavior is, without question, impeding your ability to feel free and to be the person you know you can be. It is getting in your way of being unapologetically you.

THE WORK

How would it feel to genuinely not care about what other people think?

Who would you be?

What would be different for you if you didn't take things personally?

I get it, you're saying things like "It would be amazing. I'd feel free. I could exhale. I could stop doing all the things I don't want to do. I'd say no much more often. I'd say yes much more often." The possibilities are endless, right?

> Now that you're in touch with how amazing that will feel, here are a few new thoughts I want you to practice (Practice means write it, read it, feel it.):
>
> - I am my own approval.
> - What people think of me is none of my business.
> - The more important opinion in my life is my own.

While we're still figuring out that we can survive perfectly well while we're living life our own way, we can fall into the trap of feeling like we're living someone else's life. We find ourselves doing things that we don't actually want to be doing at all.

Maybe you're doing the thing that your dad wanted you to do? Did you go along with what your peer group was doing and find yourself stuck down a path you would never have consciously chosen? If you don't feel good about the life you're living, you're not in alignment with your authentic self.

If you're living a life filled with "shoulds" and "shouldn'ts," then something has to change.

- I should go to this college.
- I should take that job; it's a good offer.
- I shouldn't travel there; it's too far.
- I should save money for a rainy day.
- I should offer group programs in my business because that's what everyone else is doing.
- I shouldn't say no when they ask for a volunteer in my kid's classroom.
- I should go because I was invited.

I have seen and heard it all. If I had a dime for every "should" I've challenged, I would be writing this book on my private island. The "shoulds" have got to go. When you stop caring what people think and you stop taking everything personally, it's easy to let go of the "shoulds" and live a life centered around making choices. YOUR choices.

When you're showing up as your best, authentic self, it's none of your business how people receive you. It's not your responsibility. I need you to hear me. You are NOT responsible for other people's reactions, perceptions, or responses. That's on them.

Say it with me again, and louder: **you are NOT responsible for other people's reactions, perceptions, or responses.**

Your life is about YOU. If you're thinking about who you are and the decisions you are choosing to make, the only opinion that matters is yours. It's not about what your kids think, what your spouse thinks, what your parents think, what your friends think, or what your siblings think; it's all about what YOU think.

If you're not being true to yourself, you are not being true to anyone.

When you care what other people think, you are literally handing them your power. "Hi, I have my own opinion, but yours is way more important than mine, so here, here's my power." Ew, no, fuck that.

It's as if their validation or opinion makes you enough or confirms your value—NO, NO, NO. Remember, your value, worthiness, and good-enoughness is NOT up for debate. Nothing that has or hasn't happened throughout your life is a reflection of your worthiness. You already have that in the bag!

Of all the wishes and wants of people I meet and work with, the biggest one is their desire to be their authentic self. There's a force within all of us that is begging us to live by our own rules, to say a guilt-free no, to stop people pleasing, to play BIG, even if it's not what the societal norm is. We have to strive to live a life that aligns with our individual truth, don't we? It sounds yummy, doesn't it?

The longer you spend creating a life seeking the acceptance of others, the further you run from your authentic self. The real, unapologetic you.

The most beautiful part of making this shift is that everyone wants to be true to themselves. We all want the same thing. So, the quicker you stop giving a shit about what everyone thinks, the quicker you stop seeking external approval and start believing that you are the only person who can offer yourself true validation. Not only will you start feeling an outrageous level of freedom and fulfillment, but you will be giving others permission to do the same.

I believe that this is one of the most miraculous by-products of your own personal growth journey. By default, you give permission to those around you to start their own journey, then that permission expands into their circles, and so on and so on and so on. Before we know it, everyone will be their unapologetic, best selves. YAY!

Let's get moving with being a catalyst for global change, shall we?

THE WORK

Repeat after me: "Don't should on me." That's right; it's your new mantra. Anytime you hear a "should" from someone else or hear it from your own mind, pause and be aware. Question the "should." Imagine it's a little should rock. Lift up the rock and see what's underneath.

- Why should or shouldn't you?
- Where does that come from?

Then shift to your power of choice and ask yourself, "Do I choose to or choose not to?"

There is no more "should." Period. ERASE it from your vocabulary.

I was at a meeting with a bunch of school moms recently, and the topic of volunteering in my kid's classroom came up. One of the moms said, "I really should make time to help in the classroom next week."

"Why should you?" I asked, daring to challenge the unwritten rules.

She immediately said, "Well, everyone else does it, and it's the kind of thing I should do because if I don't, they'll think poorly of me."

Holy shit—jackpot! What a should! This is what was under her should rock—if I don't volunteer, they won't like me.

She thought I would accept that as an answer. I carried on, "What would you like to do, you know, if you could choose?"

"I really don't want to volunteer in the classroom. I hate doing it. I don't mind the occasional field trip, but I'd much rather donate money. If I could choose, I would never volunteer in the classroom."

"Great!" I said. "I'll let you in on a little secret. You can choose. You can say no, and you can donate money instead."

The relief was palpable. She didn't volunteer. She did donate money, and she lived happily ever after. Well, I'm not sure about the last bit, but the moral of the story is that we cannot make decisions driven by shoulds. Period.

Life Sucker Number Six—Resentment

> *"Resentment is like drinking poison*
> *and waiting for the other person to die."*
> **— MALACHY MCCOURT**

Seriously, I feel like including that quote means I don't actually need to elaborate. Read it again, straight to the heart; it is such profound truth.

I remember the first time I read that quote. It struck me to my core and created an immediate shift in resentment that had been lingering in my life. I made a choice, there and then, to LET THAT SHIT GO and to stop picking it back up. It really can be that easy.

How long do you want to rot in the negativity and anger of your resentment? I'm asking you because the other person isn't being punished—you are.

Resentment can take form in a few different ways.

- **Resentment scenario one.** You are madly in love with your partner, and they are being relocated to another state. You can't imagine not being together, so you choose to move with them. You get a new job, say goodbye to your family and friends, and move to the other side of the country. Then, a few months into your new life, you start feeling easily triggered and frustrated because you are feeling resentment toward your partner. After all, they're the reason you moved, and even though it was your choice, you still feel bitter.
- **Resentment scenario two.** You have a shorter-than-short fuse with your boss. You applied for their position, but were passed up. In your eyes, your boss did you wrong, and now you are bitter; after all, you deserved that job.
- **Resentment scenario three.** You are now in a tumultuous co-parenting relationship with your ex. The same person you were once in love with now drives you to the brink of insanity just by being in the same room with you. You feel resentment toward them, among other things. The relationship didn't last, and they hurt you. Neither one of those outcomes were part of the plan when you married them.

Resentment comes when we feel a sense of injustice, even when that injustice is self-inflicted.

You might not realize that what you're feeling is resentment. If you think about an injustice that has happened in your life, you might think, "No, I let that go years ago," but if you are experiencing feelings of anger and bitterness, it's a sign you are not actually done with letting go.

THE WORK

Here's a quick resentment test. When you think of the situation, hear the person's name, or see their phone number come up on your phone, do you have a visceral reaction? Does your body contract? Do you get pissy? If you answered yes, then you still have some work to do.

Resentment is ugly. It influences terrible, harmful decision-making. It affects every aspect of your mind and body. If you are someone who is still finding it challenging to create a path of happiness, I can guarantee that resentment is buried somewhere.

Do you remember our chat about expectations? Expectations have a close relationship with resentment. If someone in your life hasn't done what you expected them to do, through your eyes, they did you wrong, and then BAM—resentment.

Do I need to underscore, again, why choosing to raise your consciousness and self-awareness is nonnegotiable? No, you've got it.

You can release resentments by choosing to put them down and stop picking them back up, by bringing awareness to what the resentment is costing you in your life, and choosing different meanings and thoughts to interpret the situation.

The truth and the most powerful way to release the chains of resentment that bind you is the single most important thing that you MUST PRACTICE in your life on the regular to achieve your potential, to experience a life of peace, joy, and fulfillment.

It's FORGIVENESS. I could write an entire book on forgiveness, and perhaps one day I will, but for now, let's just focus on the fact that implementing a forgiveness practice is nonnegotiable.

Practicing forgiveness offers freedom and peace of mind, yet so many of us choose to hold on to resentment instead. It's as if there is unwillingness to let go, an unwillingness to forgive. On some level, you must get something from the resentment you're feeling.

You could get attention. You could get a feeling of significance. You could be keeping yourself angry because that's what feels familiar to you.

THE WORK

Stop here. Connect to a feeling of resentment that you have. What do you get out of being so angry, so disconnected? As humans we don't do anything unless we're getting something out of it. If what I am saying seems outrageous to you, that doesn't make it any less true. You're getting something out of feeling like shit. Feeling angry. Feeling resentful.

Resentment eats away at your soul. It breeds an insane amount of judgment and anger, and it perpetuates a story that can actually interrupt happiness in every area of your life. It separates people in ways that you can't even wrap your mind around. It erodes relationships. It is the most toxic of all the life suckers.

So, what is stopping us from practicing forgiveness? What makes letting go so challenging?

The answers lay in our past, our beliefs. I know, shocking, our beliefs are showing up again.

Maybe we believe that by not forgiving, we will somehow achieve the justice we think we are due. We have such a deep need to be "right" that it trumps our desire to heal and be at peace. In some instances, we are under the misguided notion that forgiveness means we are condoning the situation or the other person's behavior. We might even think that if we forgive, we let the other person win.

All of these things could be true for you. Let me be clear in telling you they are all bullshit and completely not true. Those ego-driven thoughts and beliefs will keep you stuck, negative, full of resentment, and miserable for the rest of your life. Unless, of course, you choose to change your thoughts.

Allow me to tell you what forgiveness really is . . . here is the empowering belief that will lead you into a life of happiness, joy, and freedom.

Forgiveness is a GIFT. Forgiveness is a gift to yourself. When you practice forgiveness toward another person, situation, or yourself, you FREE YOURSELF. You disconnect from the burden of the past. You take back your power. You are able to live from a place of love and compassion with an open heart. You will raise your energy levels to the highest frequency. You become untouchable.

I get it: you are ready now. You don't want to drink poison for another second. Good decision!

THE WORK

Here is a powerful forgiveness practice that you can get started on this very second.

Step 1: Make a forgiveness list of people you feel have wronged you, situations where you have been hurt, and things that you'd like to forgive yourself for. Be patient and loving toward yourself as you do this work.

Step 2: Pick something or someone from your list.

Step 3: Close your eyes and for no more than two minutes picture the moment when it happened.

Step 4: See yourself and the other person or situation that hurt you. Feel the anger and the pain. Allow yourself to be vulnerable, and don't be afraid to get emotional. Stay here for about two minutes. If you feel the need to say anything out loud, do it. Don't hold back, release. Once you bring up the emotions, move to the next step.

Step 5: Forgive into love. See the person or situation in front of you, but instead of the anger, feel compassion toward them. Remembering that hurt people hurt people.

Step 6: Ask yourself, "What did I learn from this? How did this situation make me better? How did this help me grow?" Turn your focus on the person who wronged you and wonder, "What pain or anguish could they have experienced in their life that caused them to do what they did?"

Step 7: Take a few big, deep breaths. And say (to yourself or out loud), "Today I choose to forgive. I release all hurt and free myself. The more I release, the more love I have to give. Forgiveness is freeing and loving myself."

When you choose to practice ridding yourself of these life suckers, so much changes instantly. Your happiness, levity, and ease increases. Your compassion and loving kindness expands. You are far less annoyed and triggered. You can actually feel yourself becoming untouchable.

Repeat our **Worthy Human Mantra** after me:

I am worthy. I am enough. I am powerful. I get to choose.

Choice #6
ARE YOU READY TO FALL MADLY AND DEEPLY IN *Love* WITH YOURSELF?

*"You owe yourself the love you
so freely give to other people."*
— ANONYMOUS

"Love yourself." "You just have to love yourself." "Ya know, the most important thing is that you love yourself."

How many times have you heard that? Don't get me wrong; it's complete truth. But where do we start? What does that actually mean, and what does it look like when you apply it in your life?

Well, sit back and strap yourself in because shit's about to get real. I will not allow you to live one more minute of your life without LOVING YOURSELF, without liking yourself, without cultivating the relationship with yourself that you deserve. You're about to enter into a phenomenal, unconditional, accepting, and delicious relationship with yourself. Whether you are feeling some resistance to what I'm saying or reading this and shouting, "HELL YES, I AM READY," either way, it is happening.

Of course, it's still a choice. You need to choose to love yourself. For me, it's a must, because self-love IS your super power. You cannot live your best life and be your best self if you don't love yourself. It is the birthplace of your power.

So far everything we have talked about can be described as your operating system. With that in mind (literally!), think about this as your power cord. Without this essential foundation, everything else will become immobilized and impossible. Seriously, this is the driving force behind it all.

I've said it before, and I'll say it again. It's the title of the book and for good reason. Embracing and believing this opens the door for you to cultivate a deep, unconditional love of yourself. You are worthy. You are enough. You deserve love from the person who matters most in your world, YOU.

It is not debatable, negotiable, or even on the table for discussion.

You don't have to do or be anything to be enough. Are you hearing me? YOU ARE ENOUGH. YOU ARE WORTHY, simply because you woke up today. Good, now that we're back on the same page, let's dive in.

Your Lovability

Everything in your life comes from within you. Your energy, your relationships, your business, your parenting, your friendships, your choices, your connection to spirituality, everything.

Yet, I see most people focusing on everything and everyone else. They're ignoring themselves. If you picked up this book to learn new strategies in order to improve or change your life, I promise you, you will supercharge everything you have learned when you implement self-love.

I witness people "looking for love" as if someone else can create that feeling for them. I see beautiful people in loving relationships but unable to truly feel that love and let it in. Why? Because you can only feel and experience the depth of love that you have for yourself. Someone else can love you endlessly and actively, but if you don't feel your own lovability, then it doesn't matter how much you're loved from the outside in. Fucking powerful, isn't it? And it's true. Your ability to feel loved is proportionate to how lovable you believe you are and how much love you have for yourself. To love yourself is to honor, cultivate, and consistently nurture your relationship with yourself. It is the single most important relationship of your life, period. Yes, I have three awesome kids and a wonderful husband and am blessed with the most amazing family and friends. But no relationship in my life is more important than my relationship with me.

Maybe up until right now, you hadn't really considered the paradigm of a relationship with yourself, or the importance of it, at least. That's cool because you're here now and everything is about to change.

Your relationship with yourself, your love for yourself, sets the tone for your entire life. The way you treat yourself and speak to yourself creates the dynamics and thresholds for every other relationship in your life.

- Want more confidence? Love yourself.

- Ready to finally set boundaries? Love yourself.
- Time to go after that dream? Love yourself.
- Need to have that crucial conversation? Love yourself.
- Want to have the romantic relationship of your dreams? Love yourself.
- Ready to release your emotion? Love yourself.
- Want to create space and find ease? Love yourself.

Yes, it's the answer because everything starts with you.

There isn't one thing that defines "loving yourself" or a quick "how to" that defines what a phenomenal relationship with yourself looks like. It's several components that you choose to become aware of moment to moment. Every. Single. Day.

Your relationship with yourself requires attention and nurturing the same way any other relationship does.

To embrace all of this, let's move through the areas of self-love one at a time. Knowing that these areas make up the relationship you have with yourself, you can choose to practice them, and in doing so, you will be well on your way to deeply and unconditionally loving yourself.

#1: Self-Acceptance

Your relationship with yourself starts with self-acceptance.

Self-acceptance means that you are able to embrace and accept all facets of yourself. I'm not just talking about the positive, more "desirable" parts of yourself; I'm talking about every single element of who you are. From a place of self-acceptance, you can recognize weaknesses, imperfections, and missteps without judgment and without any interference when it comes to accepting yourself.

Your ability to accept yourself in this moment will have been influenced by how accepted you were as a child. Before the age of seven or eight, we don't even have a sense of self at all, so we are reliant on what is transmitted to us through the people who raise us.

If you were brought up in an environment that transmitted unconditional acceptance of you and your behaviors, you are likely to have an easier time accepting yourself in this moment. Conversely, if the people who raised you transmitted that they were unwilling or unable to accept every aspect of you, then this one might take some extra time and practice, but that's okay; this is your time to choose.

No matter where you land on the upbringing spectrum, we all experience an amount of being conditionally accepted. This means that you believe you can only accept yourself if you behave in a predefined way.

Six-year-old Megan lived with her mom and younger brother. She was the model sister and genuinely loved her brother, which was a relief to her mom. After school, she would drag her toy box into the middle of her room and invite her brother in to play with her.

"You're such a good girl, Megan, you are so generous, and I love you for helping to entertain your brother," her mom would say as she walked past the room. "Look, you're making him so happy! I love you for doing that."

Being the grown-up six-year-old that she was, sometimes Megan wanted to play by herself. After a long day at school, she craved some time to play with her favorite toys, uninterrupted. "Can I play by myself for a few minutes please, Mom?" she pleaded.

"That's not very nice; that means your brother will have to play by himself, and good girls know how to share."

Day after day, Megan heard the same message. If she was being "good," as defined by her mom, then she was lovable. We all know that a girl needs her downtime, so Megan wasn't asking for anything she didn't need and deserve, yet that request was denied with the message that she wasn't "good," that she was unlovable. Growing up, Megan believed that in order to be accepted, she would have to please other people and ignore her own needs.

———

Eric was the youngest of four children. His parents were both scientists, and he watched as his siblings grew up, excelled at school, and dreamed of living the academic high life. He would sit at the dinner table, listening every day to his parents praise his siblings, discuss their latest grades, and plan how they were going to change the world with their genius.

"How has your day been, Eric?" That fateful question. It wasn't that his parents weren't interested; they just didn't know how to praise someone who preferred drawing the sunset to explaining the science behind why it happened.

"Fine, thanks." What else could he say? He didn't want to admit that despite hours of studying he still failed his math exam, but he had directed a piece of interpretive dance that had resulted in his teacher presenting him with the Class Oscar.

Eric received the same message every day. He learned that unless he was book smart, he was a failure. Acceptance was conditional and based on academic prowess. He felt a level of shame about his creativity because it was glossed over at best but usually ignored by his family.

Dependent acceptance creates a profound level of negativity that is often found as the root cause of issues that travel with us into adulthood. The judgments and harsh criticisms that we repeat to ourselves have been on a loop for years, influencing our decision-making.

Here's the thing: none of that is real or true. None of it. It's just what you believed up until now, but right now, in this moment, you can believe something different.

You can believe the truth. You are perfectly imperfect, as every human is.

Your relationship with yourself begins with total, unconditional acceptance of every amazing, not-so-amazing, and neutral part of you because together, they make up the person you are today. Yummy, worthy you.

You can choose to forgive yourself for the judgments, and you can silence your unhelpful inner critic. In order to truly accept yourself, you need to forgive yourself. Forgive those missteps that you've made along the journey of your life, forgive yourself for the things that didn't work out the way you'd hoped, forgive yourself for not being exactly where you wanted to be by this stage in your life. If there's anything in your life that is clouded in shame or guilt, forgive yourself and set yourself free.

THE WORK

Write this down and read it out loud every day: I accept myself, fully and unconditionally. I am worthy, whole, and enough.

If at first that feels like too much of a stretch, you can start with: I am willing to start fully and unconditionally accepting myself. I am worthy, whole, and enough.

In time, with repetition and through choosing your new belief, you will accept every part of your delicious self.

This is a practice and a process; it's not an overnight shift nor does it need to be. Simply being here, reading this book, is an incredible first step in choosing and accepting yourself. You will get there, I promise. Take one step and make one choice at a time.

#2: Self-Compassion

Self-compassion is one of the most beautiful components of your relationship with yourself. It means being patient, kind, gentle, and sympathetic toward yourself and to do unto yourself that which you would naturally do for someone else. Seriously, when was the last time you were calm, patient, and gentle with yourself when something went wrong, when you didn't feel your best, or show up as your best self?

Exactly. It has been way too long.

To have self-compassion means you're choosing kindness. Whenever you're feeling unsure, unable to process what's happening, something didn't go the way you intended for it to go, or you're not showing up as your best self, you can ask yourself, "What do I need in this moment?" The same way you would if you saw that your BFF was struggling. Instead of choosing judgment or chastising yourself for not coping and dealing with everything like a pro, choose kindness. If you don't, you'll only exacerbate your negative emotions around the situation.

Self-compassion means no more isolation, no more thinking that you're alone, because you're not. We are all connected, and we all have common human experiences. When you isolate yourself, you're not showing yourself compassion. You know when you're facing self-imposed isolation because you're thinking, "It's just me," "This shouldn't be happening," "Something went wrong," or "Something is wrong with me."

Alana, the powerhouse, was a perfectionist and overachiever. There was nothing this woman couldn't do, and to the outside world, she was taking it all in stride. She was a fierce businesswoman, a mother of toddler twin girls, and a philanthropist in her community.

"She never stops, she's so generous, she'll do anything for anyone, and she's always on top of it. Don't mess with her, though; she didn't get to where she is in life by being a pushover."

Alana came to her session overwhelmed. She started right in: "I'm exhausted and totally embarrassed. The girls are wearing me out. They threw tantrums when we were out yesterday; it was so embarrassing. I lost my shit."

"What happened?" I asked.

"We were checking out at the grocery store, and they were grabbing gum off the register, and when I said no, they threw themselves down on the floor of the store and were screaming. I lost it and screamed. I was mortified and couldn't get out of there fast enough. So embarrassing! What kind of mother am I if I can't even keep my own kids under control?" she exclaimed. "And what must the people at the store think of me? I can't show my face in there anytime soon."

"Let's take a deep breath," I said. "The only thing that is making this so terrible is the way you're looking at it. The way you are being to yourself.

"Do you know of other parents of singles, never mind twins, whose toddlers don't act like toddlers? Have you never seen anyone else's kids throw tantrums?"

"Of course, kids will be kids. But I should be able to control mine. And you should have seen how embarrassing it was. It's not okay," she argued.

"Imagine you saw another mom going through this exact scenario. What would you be thinking?"

"I'd probably feel bad for her and want to tell her she's not alone because I know how it feels!"

"Yup, now take it one step further. Your best friend calls you and tells you a similar story about her kids. How do you respond?"

"I'd tell her I love her, she's an amazing mom. Parenting is not easy, and she's doing a great job. And to put the kids to bed early and do something nice for herself, like take a bath or have a phone date with me."

"Exactly. So, what's stopping you from being supportive and compassionate to yourself, the same way you just explained you'd be with others?" I asked.

"I don't have a good answer. I'm used to being hard on myself. I feel like pushing myself is how I've gotten where I am. I'm starting to realize that it doesn't feel so good."

"It's time for some self-compassion. This is something you choose, so you can learn to be as kind and loving toward yourself as you would be to anyone else. You are the most important relationship in your life. You need to treat yourself that way."

The tears started to fall down her cheeks. "I know. I want to be so much nicer to me. I will be. Not only do I want it for myself, but I also want my girls to see it."

I cried a little too. I usually do. Experiencing moments of realization never gets old for me.

Self-compassion is a moment-to-moment choice. You need to understand that the person you are addressing is the most important person in your life, so act accordingly.

THE WORK

All you have to do is relate to yourself in the same way you would to your best friend. When you are experiencing a moment of suffering, misfortune, perceived failure, or pain, become your own

> best friend. Think about the words you're using, the tone of those words, and ask yourself, "What do I need right now?"
>
> "How can I be gentle and kind to myself in this moment?"
>
> "What can I do to embrace my beautiful human-ness and remind myself I'm not alone?"

Then, choose to listen to the answer.

You are the most important relationship of your life. Treat yourself as such.

#3: Self-Talk

Have you ever really stopped to notice the way you talk to yourself? Well, by the time we're done here, you will become astutely aware of the shit you say to yourself, whether it's in your mind or out loud.

That's what self-talk is, plain and simple: it's the way you talk to yourself. And after noticing this for myself and working with countless other incredible souls to do the same, I can tell you in no uncertain terms that you wouldn't dare speak to someone you love, or even someone you don't love, the way you talk to yourself.

> It was a Friday night, our children were being taken care of, and my husband, David, and I were getting ready for a party. It wasn't just any party; this was a special celebration for one of our closest friends. We had been looking forward to it for weeks, but now that the time had come, I didn't want to go.

"Ugh," I said, standing in front of the mirror, checking out the outfit I had chosen for the occasion.

"Ugh, what?" came a shout from the bathroom.

"Ugh, I'm chunky and this is not cute," I said, pointing at the image staring back at me.

Marching out of the bathroom, toothbrush in hand, David looked into the mirror with me, and said, "Nope, that is unacceptable. Don't talk to yourself like that," before marching back into the bathroom to continue getting ready.

He told me!

The word "chunky" was just the shit that I was spewing in my own head. I know better than that, but I needed the reminder.

No wonder I didn't want to go. It's impossible to feel good if you're saying horrible things to yourself.

That moment led to a higher state of awareness about my own self-talk. You can't forget about being consciously aware just because it's a Friday night and you're going out.

Did that story resonate with you, or do any of these sound familiar?

- You're so stupid.
- You suck at this.
- Who do you think you are?
- You're too fat.

- Who's going to love you?
- You're not good enough.
- You are forgettable.
- You are constantly making mistakes.
- WTF is wrong with you?
- You fucked that up.
- You're not that smart.

Ew. I feel less-than and shitty just typing it out.

But the truth is, so many of us are moving through life with that kind of soundtrack playing in our heads. We're doing it to ourselves. That's fucking insane, right?

There's plenty to deal with and manage outside of you without you choosing to fight against yourself. It's simply unacceptable.

You are your own person, and that person needs to be your rock, your cheerleader, your fan club. That person needs to show up with compassion and kindness. That person needs to offer empowering words of wisdom.

Your mind communicates with you in images and words every second of every day, and right now, we're going to concentrate on choosing the words that will serve us.

It's time to make praise familiar. Now, you know that your mind loves what's familiar and resists what's unfamiliar. It's science. We've already talked that through.

The reason why it's so easy to continue the habit of judgmental and critical self-talk is because you've been doing it for so long, it's all your mind is familiar with.

To feel the way you want to feel, to be who you want to be, and to create what you want to create in this world, getting comfortable with praise and empowering self-talk is essential.

Nothing is more important than the words you say to yourself.

THE WORK

Pause here, take a deep breath. Now read this out loud if you can: "You're amazing. I love you so much. You are enough and you are lovable. You're the cutest. You are destined for success. Mistakes are how you learn. There's nothing you can't do. You're awesome at figuring things out. You are a worthy human."

Feels amazing, right? That's what loving, empowering self-talk feels like.

Our self-talk comes from our past. Shocking, I know. It's habitual, and until you shine a light on it, you won't recognize how damaging it is. Some of the negative self-talk you notice might even sound like your parents, siblings, or teachers. If you notice statements like "Go brush you hair, it looks crazy," "Your thighs are too big," or "You talk too much," you might be able to attribute them to their original source.

But the original source doesn't matter because you're a grown-ass human who takes Radical Personal Responsibility and lives in the power of your own choices, so we are going to cut this shit out, right now.

Your voice is the most important voice in your life. Building a phenomenal relationship with yourself means being president of your own fan club. And that means choosing positive, loving, compassionate self-talk.

THE WORK

Let's play with this.

- Grab a piece of paper, turn it horizontally, and draw a line down the middle.
- On the top of the left side write "Shitty Committee," and on the top of the right side write "Fan Club."

VOICE OF JUDGEMENT
SHITTY COMMITTEE

Ugh. You're so fat.
I hate you so much.
You'll never measure up.
Everyone hates you.
Too stupid.
Idiot.
You suck!
Loser.
Weak.
You never have enough money.
Ugly!
Who could ever love you?
You'll never be good at this.
Failure.

VOICE OF WISDOM
FAN CLUB

You are Loved ♡
Look how far you've come.
Awesome + Amazing!
You're gorgeous!
You're Special.
Incredible!
You are brilliant.
Strong!
Powerful
BADASS
You're a ROCKSTAR
You are enough.
I love you!

- Draw a stick figure on each side of the page, or if you're fabulously creative, draw yourself in detail; you choose!
- Give each side a name, but they have to be names that ARE NOT linked to anyone you know!
- Then, draw word bubbles around each figure representing what they usually say to you. The Shitty Committee might say things

like "You suck. You never finish anything. You are so stupid. No one's going to like you." The Fan Club might say things like "You look amazing. I love you. You did so well. You are so generous."

As you bring awareness to your self-talk, when you hear your Shitty Committee, you can choose to listen to your fan club instead. Address them by name, engage with them, and choose who you want to have in your corner.

You are too amazing, too worthy, and too fucking awesome to be mean to yourself.

#4: Self-Care

How you care for yourself is a component of the health and nourishment of your relationship with yourself. In truth, every component of loving yourself is caring for yourself.

I believe that self-love IS self-care. Because when you fully and unconditionally love yourself, you will inherently care for yourself. So, the more of this work you apply, the quicker self-care will become your new default.

Self-care is caring for yourself physically, emotionally, and spiritually.

Your physical self-care is all about caring for your body, your vessel. Your emotional self-care is all about allowing, expressing, and embracing your feelings. Your spiritual self-care is all about your connection to something greater than you and nourishing your soul. With each element, you get to choose how to care for yourself in the best possible way.

For the sake of our journey together, there are three key concepts that I want to share that fall under deep, nourishing self-care. These are: prioritizing yourself, prioritizing your boundaries, and allowing yourself to feel your feelings. True self-care goes way beyond a spa day.

PRIORITIZING YOURSELF

It's insane that I even need to write this, but you really do have to be the priority in your own life.

Can you please stop creating a world where you are last on the list every damn day?

So many people insist on trying to please everyone else, making themselves the last thing on the totem pole of their life. They make sure that everything and everyone in the universe has been tended to before they think about what they want or need. That's if they think about themselves at all.

You know what I'm talking about: saying yes to everything, carrying the weight of the world on your shoulders, compromising yourself, letting other people impact your self-worth . . . it's all got to go!

How long can you keep pouring your energy into doing everything for everyone else? Keep it up, and before you know it, you'll be so drained and so exhausted, so full of resentment, that you have made yourself ill. Yes, you will have done it to yourself.

I am begging you to reverse the belief that everyone else takes priority. They do not.

Amy was the queen of the reversed totem pole. She was at the bottom, her face barely even carved in the wood. Her day started at five o'clock, when she would catch up on the things her boss had deemed critical as she was leaving the office the day before. Before waking her three children, she would prepare their breakfast and lunch, hand her husband a freshly made coffee on his way out, and then start the monumental task of completing the school run. After nine o'clock, things really got busy! You know how it goes.

"I'm not sleeping, Tracy."

In fairness, she didn't need to tell me that. She looked exhausted. I was tempted to cancel our session, make her a chamomile tea, and invite her to nap for the hour.

"It takes me ages to get to sleep because I'm thinking about all the things I didn't get finished. I'm probably on a bit of a sugar and caffeine high because I have been trying to stay awake all day, and then when I finally get to sleep, it feels like I have ten minutes to sleep before the alarm goes off and I start all over again."

When I dared mention the words "self-care," she responded as if I was holding a gun to her head, demanding that she hand over everything she valued.

"What would they all do without me? They need my help. I'll be fine. If I took time out to do something for myself, I'd have even more to do when I got home. My mom was fine, and she looked after everyone and everything. I mean, she seemed happy. At least I think she was happy."

Amy stopped talking and looked like she had seen a ghost. "I'm trying to be like my mom, but she isn't here anymore. She missed out on so much. She was busy in the kitchen while we ate, she was tidying the house while we played—she was looking after us, and nobody was looking after her. She needed to be needed, and I'm doing exactly the same thing."

"Yes, yes you are. That was an awesome realization, and now it's time to make some new choices because of it," I explained.

From that moment, Amy made different choices. She saved her own life. Amy started choosing to sleep in a little later and allowed the work to be handled during her actual workday. She chose to get up before the kids and have time for herself: time to drink coffee, time to journal, time to just be without anyone needing anything from her. She started asking for help dropping the kids at school, and between herself, her husband, and carpooling with friends, she actually added time to her day. Amy also decided to make time to exercise a few times a week and prioritize her nutrition.

As a result of her new choices, she created new results. She was sleeping better, more present in all areas of her life, and she was happier. And she learned the world didn't fall apart and that everyone was more than okay without her being everything to everyone.

And yes, she has to consciously choose, moment-to-moment, day-to-day. Because you always have to choose. With each choice, she felt better and better.

The irony of all this is that you believe that prioritizing everything and everyone else shows the world that you're a valuable human being. It doesn't. When you put everything and everyone else first, no one is getting the best version of you because you haven't cared for yourself enough to have the energy to offer your best self to all the beautiful people and blessings you have in your life.

Who is refueling YOU? The answer is YOU need to refuel you. You're the only person who can do this, and you can start now by prioritizing yourself.

Take the same advice that you're given by the airlines and transfer it into your own everyday choices. Every time you fly, you're told that if there's an emergency, you must place the oxygen mask on yourself FIRST before helping others. You cannot help anyone if you don't have enough oxygen. It really is that simple.

So, it's my honor to introduce to you the concept of "healthy selfish." Healthy selfish means to prioritize yourself so you can enjoy, honor, and engage in all of the different areas of your life. Healthy selfish is guilt-free and is a vital component of building a phenomenal relationship with yourself.

THE WORK

Ready to start prioritizing yourself and become healthy selfish?

Make a long list of things that refuel you, a "me time" list. Each week, pick at least three things from the list, schedule them in, make them nonnegotiable, and choose YOU!

Say it with me: "I am healthy selfish!"

BOUNDARIES

Take a deep breath. You've got this! Setting and exercising boundaries will change your life.

I feel that there are a lot of misconceptions around boundaries. This is the way I choose to understand them: my personal boundaries are simply defining what I am willing to do and what I am not willing to do. It's simple, and it works. This is what I am available for; this is what I'm not available for.

Your ability to set and honor your boundaries is a direct reflection of how you value the relationship you have with yourself, how you value your own self-worth. I know it sounds harsh, but hearing the truth will help you change. Let's be honest, when have I ever shied away from being harsh?

You might have tried to set and uphold boundaries in the past or perhaps attempted to shift your boundaries based on a certain relationship or situation. That doesn't work because the boundary becomes about the other person or the situation rather than about what you are willing to do and not willing to do.

The truth is, the only people that will have issues with your boundaries are the people who were benefitting from you not having any.

Setting and upholding boundaries is crucial for your well-being. We need to set boundaries to practice self-love and self-respect, to communicate our needs, to improve interactions, and to make time and space for ourselves.

So, what makes setting and defining boundaries such a difficult thing to do? It could be that you were raised in a home that had no boundaries, so you never were taught that it was an option for you. It could be your own fears lurking in the background, a fear of rejection if you say no or tell someone how you feel.

The truth is, boundaries are love. Love for the boundary setter and love for the person receiving the boundary.

Regardless of where you currently stand on setting and upholding your own boundaries, you're not leaving our time together as the same person you were when we started. You're upgrading, and this upgrade requires boundaries.

THE WORK

The best way to identify where you need a boundary or where you need to re-enforce an old boundary is by checking in on where you feel frustrated, resentful, or depleted.

Consider the areas of your life, the relationships in your life.

- Where are you leaking energy?
- Where do you feel tired?
- What are you tolerating that you no longer want to tolerate?
- Where are you easily triggered and reactive?

Once you've identified that, you can construct and decide what boundaries you are committing to.

If you're still not feeling pumped about the boundaries you will create for yourself, know this: the more healthy and aligned boundaries you set and uphold, the closer you will get to living your truth. The closer you move toward your unapologetic self and igniting your personal power. The more energy you will have to show up fully for yourself and all the magnificence in your life.

FEEL YOUR FEELINGS

I cannot think of anything that shows you're caring for yourself more than embracing your yummy, mushy emotions.

If you were raised in a family where emotion was taboo, if you were told crying is weakness, or you were laughed at when you tried to articulate your feelings, you might have promised yourself you would never show your vulnerable side again. If you were told that you were showing off because you were proud of something you achieved or ridiculed for your positivity, you might harbor the belief that these emotions are something to be ashamed of.

Do you see how your beliefs are showing up EVERYWHERE?

Whatever or whoever gifted you this approach, it is not serving you today. It is not supporting your journey toward a life of happiness, joy, and fulfillment.

It's time to stop hiding and start embracing. Recognizing and feeling your emotions are both part of the human experience.

Emotions are a natural and beautiful gift. Plain and simple. Emotions can be indicators that something is wrong or that something is right. Either way, they act as an indicator that it's time to discover what's going on for us.

I want you to feel your feelings. Let that excitement flow. Exude your pride and happiness until your face hurts from smiling. Radiate with joy and exuberance about your amazing self.

We are designed to feel. We were not built to suppress, bury, or hide our emotions because when we do, it results in a volcano-like explosion or physical illness. That's a pretty clear sign there's a problem, but you don't need to wait for a system failure to know there's a problem.

Crying and laughing are forms of emotion that allow energy to be released from the body. They are the most popular form of decongestant for your emotional blockage; it's time to let it up and out!

I happen to be a big fan of a long, deep cry. It's most effective when you're curled up in the fetal position on the floor, snot bubbles and all . . . try it and you'll feel like you have lost one hundred pounds of baggage.

It's time to give yourself permission to feel your feelings, to talk about how you feel, whether you're in the pits of despair or over-the-moon with happiness, and everything in between. It's always better out than in.

When you are comfortable and cool with feeling any and all emotions, you deepen your untouchability and your confidence.

THE WORK

Start with giving yourself permission to feel your feelings.

When you feel sadness and tears coming up, do not suppress or push them down. Remind yourself that everything is better up and out, and allow yourself to cry. Allow yourself to go there and feel the release.

Feeling the need to release some energy, perhaps even some pent-up anger? Go into a private room or the garage (that's my spot of choice), and scream at the top of your lungs. Horror-movie style.

When someone asks you how you're feeling, be honest and express yourself.

Emotion is expression. Emotion is human. Whatever emotion is coming up for you, LOVE YOURSELF and choose to feel it.

#5: Self-Image

Our final component of fully loving ourselves is our self-image, how we see ourselves.

This one is HUGE because you will always stay within the constructs of this vision of how you see yourself and what you believe about yourself.

The awesomeness of everything we're doing together underscores the fact that you are not fixed. You are not bound by the limitations that have been placed on you, by yourself or others, and you can change how you choose to see yourself. You are a worthy, limitless being!

At the start of this book, we talked about how you reached this stage of your life and how you developed the identity you have today.

Now, you get to practice the power of choosing what you believe about your identity. You get to decide who you want to be, how you want to feel, how you want to show up in the world. You get to design your own self-image!

To start, think about all the things you say that are followed by "That's just the way I am."

- I'm a neat freak; that's just the way I am.
- I get nervous in a big group; that's just the way I am.
- I'm always late; that's just the way I am.
- I take things personally; that's just the way I am.
- I struggle with confidence; that's just the way I am.
- I'm not talented in anything; that's just the way I am.
- I'm ugly; that's just the way I am.
- I'm not smart; that's just the way I am.
- I don't have a creative bone in my body; that's just the way I am.
- I'm not good enough; that's just the way I am.

Here's the thing: it's not just the way you are. It's just the way you THINK you are. WHAT? It's okay, take a moment and read that line over and over until it sinks in.

That's not to say that you aren't experiencing those concepts or behaviors as true. You are. You're always late, you're a neat freak, and you struggle with confidence, but not because they are your truth; it's because we always live up to or down to our self-image.

You are not fixed. When you change your thoughts, beliefs, and stories, you change your self-image.

It's not about the way you think you are. It is about what is

relevant in this moment. Who do you need to be in this very moment to feel, be, do, and create everything you want in your life?

Remember, you are lovable, you are enough, you are worthy, and you CAN choose to change your self-image.

Your self-talk might be going crazy with resistance right now, and that's okay. You can choose to change that too.

Say this out loud: "I am lovable, I am enough, I am worthy." Then listen for the little voices that talk back to you in your head. What did you hear? If you heard "No, you're not. Who are you kidding?" That's the resistance. That's the disempowering voice of judgment we talked about earlier.

You can choose loving self-talk instead. That sounds like "You're right. You are enough. You are lovable. All the shit you used to believe, you don't believe it anymore. You get to choose."

When it comes to self-image, you get to decide exactly who you want to be. You can break up with parts of yourself that don't serve you and cultivate new parts that do. Woohoo! I know, it's like you have just won the lottery!

When you start practicing self-love, you automatically start to shift your self-image. When you change your self-image, EVERY-THING starts to change.

It really is time to embrace the fact that the most important relationship you will ever have in your life is the relationship you have with yourself. Loving yourself is such an incredibly powerful, nonnegotiable choice that I want to share a couple more practical ideas to help you along the way.

THE WORK

- Get a dry erase marker and write "I AM ENOUGH" on every mirror in your house. Make sure you include the mirror in the bathroom.
- Mirror work is profound; it cultivates a nurturing relationship with yourself. Thanks to Louise Hay, the pioneer of this work, I start my day by going to the mirror, looking myself in the eyes, and I saying, "I love you."
- Take the time to fall in love with yourself. Grab a bottle of wine, a movie, and spend the evening with yourself, take yourself to dinner, date yourself.

Finally, this is the perfect place to share my guiding life questions with you. Thinking about and answering these questions will help you actively love yourself, honor your worth, and choose yourself.

Use them anytime you don't feel how you want to feel or in a moment where you know you aren't making the best choice for your life. Perhaps in a situation where you want to connect to yourself and make a choice from a space of honor and self-love. Use these. They will help, every time.

- What would this situation look like if I loved myself right now?
- Who would I be in this moment if I believed I was enough?
- How does this serve me?

Repeat our **Worthy Human Mantra** after me:

I am worthy. I am enough. I am powerful. I get to choose.

Choice #7
ARE YOU READY TO GIVE YOURSELF PERMISSION TO BE *Happy?*

"Happiness is not out there, it's in you."

— ANONYMOUS

Happiness. Happiness. Happiness. Isn't happiness what we're all after? Isn't happiness the point?

I believe that happiness is the feeling that we are all chasing. Whether you call it joy, satisfaction, bliss, or contentment, we're all chasing that feeling.

We set goals because we think once we reach them we'll be happy. We change jobs because we think something new will make us happy. We date in the hopes of meeting our life partner so we can be happy. We start businesses to have the freedom to do things our own way so we can be happy. We have kids because the joy of parenting will make us happy. I laugh as I write this one because as a mother of three, I can assure you that the "joy of parenting" does not always make me happy.

When you drill it down, the choices we make are based on chasing the feeling of happiness. It's **the thing** we all are searching for.

Happiness First

What are we waiting for? Happiness is available now. It's not something unobtainable, something we have to wait for, or something we have to hand over money to achieve; we can be happy NOW. Like right now. You can CHOOSE happy! The way you feel is a choice.

We were raised to think of happiness as something we get as a reward. If we achieved something, we would be compensated with something that made us happy. So, we have to earn happiness, right? WRONG! We were raised to believe that happiness is a by-product of our external circumstances, and as a result, some of these thoughts may sound familiar:

- As soon as I lose this weight, then I'll be happy.
- When I score that big client, then I'll be happy.
- When I find the love of my life, then I'll be happy.
- When I get two thousand followers on social media, then I'll be happy.
- Once my kids are older and sleep through the night, then I'll be happy.
- When my partner and I stop fighting, then I'll finally be happy.

So, after all of those external variables, you'll finally give yourself the permission to be happy? No, thank you. That paradigm is outdated, limited, and total bullshit.

Living in an "if, then" happiness paradigm leaves you never satisfied, always chasing the next thing, and totally dependent on the last good or bad thing that happened to you.

Your happiness, as with all of your other feelings, comes from within you. When you choose a reward-based paradigm, not only will it be much harder to achieve the things you want, but you will also set yourself up for a life that is only as happy as the last thing that went your way. It will be a life based on your external circumstances, and that is no way to live. It definitely won't be a life of embracing your personal responsibility and vast inner power.

In order to live a life that you love, happiness has to come first.

Happiness Is a State

Although we touched on lower-self and higher-self states earlier in our journey (your glass elevator), we are going to take a look at it again because your states and feelings *are* your inner environment and because your mind loves repetition.

There are two basic states: lower-self, disempowering states and higher-self, empowering states.

Here's an at-a-glance list of the emotions and feelings that fall under each.

Lower-Self/Disempowering States

Anger, Impatience, Anxiety, Judgment, Comparison, Stress, Overwhelm, Indecision, Envy, Depression, Powerlessness, Disappointment, Worry, Frustration, Self-Doubt, Negativity

Higher-Self/Empowering States

Happiness, Joy, Ease, Peace, Compassion, Love, Gratitude, Confidence, Excitement, Courage, Calmness, Flow, Faith, Curiosity, Allowing, Openness, Patience, Optimism, Vulnerability

Right now, you're probably assessing which type of inner environment you spend more time in. Maybe even having an "aha" moment as you see it laid out in front you so clearly.

THE WORK

Check in with yourself. How many hours of your day do you spend in disempowering states? How many hours of your day do you spend in empowering states?

The bottom line is the more hours of each day that you spend in higher-self states, the happier you will be. And the happier you are, the more you are able to access your creativity, sprinkle in levity, take inspired action, and attract and create a life you are madly in love with.

So far on our journey together, we have explored the fact that our thoughts create our feelings and that our feelings influence our thoughts. There's an ongoing tennis match between our thoughts and feelings, with each side being both reactionary and providing direction depending on which one is feeling stronger on any given day.

While this game of tennis will continue indefinitely, you can step in and be the awareness umpire. You can become aware of any thoughts or feelings that are not resulting in your happiness. You get to choose whether or not you want to experience happiness in that moment and use your power of choice to make it happen.

This does mean that you have to take back your power and take responsibility for your state of happiness. If you don't, you're allowing yourself to be a victim of your external circumstances. If you have chosen to be happy, you have to make the choices that allow your thoughts and feelings to remain in alignment with that decision.

Got it? Good.

Choose Happiness

Why would you choose to feel like shit on purpose? If happiness is the goal, what are you doing to feel it? You do want to feel happy, right?

You have conditioned your mind and body to believe that happiness is something that is achieved due to your external circumstances. You're feeding your mind and body the thought that happiness can only exist for you when you have done something to deserve it. If you are still living in a low-self state, then of course, you'll never deserve it. Your internal dialogue won't allow you to believe that you deserve it, and it will be impossible for you to experience happiness. In your low-self state, happiness is unfamiliar.

Life on level two isn't about happiness; it's about basking in the familiarity of negativity, so your well-trodden neuropathways will revert to the route they know best, seeking happiness by external means but never achieving it.

Do you see how the pursuit of happiness is actually contributing to making us profoundly unhappy? The fucking irony! Everything you have learned so far will have laid the foundations to show you that you can change your inner environment and consciously choose happiness, right now. When you start to feel the twinges of unfamiliarity, it's just biology in action. It's not a sign from the universe that you don't deserve happiness. Through repeatedly choosing happiness, you are creating a familiar pathway by making the unfamiliar familiar, and through commitment and consistency, you can be happy NOW.

Melissa had hit a wall. "I'll never get there. I'll never be happy," she told me after we had been working together for a couple of months.

She had been committed to the process: raising her awareness, noticing the shifts in her behavior, and starting her days by making a choice about how she was going to feel that day.

"What choice are you making?" I asked, curious about why she was struggling.

"I say, 'Today I choose to be happy.' I let go of worry, and I choose to be happy. But sometimes I still have thoughts of worry that come in. I feel like I was doing so great on choosing happy, but it's hard to change. Why won't the worry stop completely?"

I couldn't help but smile. "Melissa, you have spent over forty years conditioning your body, your cells, to respond and be fueled by thoughts and feelings of worry and negativity. They aren't interested in changing what they have known their whole life. Right now, all of those cells are starting to change. Because you, the being in charge, is starting to change. That's fucking amazing, by the way.

"Imagine all of those little cells busy worrying, feeling negative and stressed, are cartoon characters that talk to one another. They've been hanging out, familiar with the daily directive of worry or nega- tivity, and now, all of a sudden, there's a new directive. Our little cell friends don't like change. They feel sick, they're not getting their daily dose of familiarity, and they decide to hold an urgent, man- datory meeting. That meeting turns into a protest and they form a picket line, refusing to follow the new choice of happiness and ease. They want to know what the fuck you're doing up there. Where is the worry, negativity, and stress that they have been nourished by their whole life? Happiness and ease are new, and they don't like it one bit. It is a threat to their survival."

This is what makes your commitment to change and your power of choice so important. Your mind and those cells don't know what you want, but you do. You are the one with all the power.

Melissa is someone who started her personal growth journey a long time ago. Even though these choices seem obvious when they're pointed out to you, it's not easy to practice them on a daily basis. It's simple, but not easy.

Melissa can create deep, sustainable change by continuing to raise her awareness, continuing to use her happiness like a guidance system, then pausing to redirect her thoughts from her default thinking to her new chosen thoughts. Thinking on purpose. Consciously choosing to make the unfamiliar, familiar. Over time, she will have reconditioned herself to be the way she wants to be, feel the way she wants to feel. Her desired way will now be her default. Ahhhhhh. Amazing.

You have been conditioned to believe that happiness is reward based for decades. You have been reading this book for, well, I don't know how long, but it will be significantly less than decades. You are doing your best, and choosing happiness may go against everything you have been conditioned to believe, up until now.

Keep choosing. Keep taking Radical Personal Responsibility because before you know it, these new feelings become your automatic, default way of being. Yes, for real.

The work works when you work it, 100 percent of the time.

The Happiness Catalyst

When you choose happiness and higher-self states, you feel happy and you access more creativity.

When you are happy, you are open, you are relaxed, you are in flow. Your brain is online and engaged. You're in the sweet spot for creativity.

Conversely, when you are low and under stress, your fight or flight response is active. This causes the amygdala to shut down brain operation in preparation for survival, not the optimal environment for creative thinking.

Happiness is a catalyst to feeling connected to yourself and your intuition. Happiness feels good and influences you to take inspired action in every aspect of your life.

The way you feel influences what you choose to do or choose not to do. So, choosing happiness makes sense, right?

If you have chosen happiness, it will propel your business forward. Taking inspired action means you'll have more to offer your clients, you'll feel empowered to speak on stage, you'll write your book, you'll enthusiastically share your message with the world.

If you have chosen happiness, you will feel inspired to plan a romantic night with your partner. You'll enjoy shopping for a sexy outfit and feel fabulous when you wear it. You'll be focusing on spending time together and connecting.

We don't need to describe what happens in your business or your relationship when you don't choose happiness, as you no doubt have experienced this. You are always the problem, and you are always the solution.

If you liked the sound of the happiness catalyst business model or happiness catalyst relationship model, you know what you need to do. Start with the choice. Raise your energy and be your higher self. As a direct result, you will make inspired choices that lead to, yup, you guessed it, more happiness and more of what you want.

YOU can be the catalyst for happiness for the people around you too. We've all been in situations where the energy is unmistakably negative. You know what I mean, when someone walks into a meeting and it feels like the air has been sucked out of the room and replaced with a palpable heaviness. Conversely, there are people who walk into a meeting and immediately you feel better. You experience the shift, you feel inspired and lighter. Which person would you prefer to be?

You can choose to be a catalyst for happiness anytime you like. All you have to do is smile at a stranger, dance in the line at the grocery store (yes, I do that, don't you?). You can choose to be so fucking joyful that people look at you and want what you're having.

Not-So-Seriously Happy?

I know what you're thinking: "We can't always feel happy; that's not realistic." You're completely correct. That is not the goal here. We're humans, and we all have human experiences. Those experiences lead to a range of feelings and emotions, each and every one of which is a gift.

This is not about being told to think positively or being a fake-happy version of yourself. That's not authentic. This is not about rainbows, unicorns, and sprinkling glitter.

Shit happens, and when it happens, you absolutely recognize and honor what you're feeling, but you don't stay there. You don't choose to live there. You choose to engage in and evaluate what has happened, determining if something needs to be healed, deciding if it gets any fucks, and then surrender back into your happiness.

You get to choose which floor you visit and how long you would like to stay there. You deserve the twenty-ninth floor, and yes, it is totally possible to live there. It is totally within your power to make the choices that will create a state of being that blows your own mind!

Just like when you're dancing in the line at the grocery store, you need to be able to let go of your inherent seriousness. Let go of the intensity and the self-inflicted pressure. Yes, all pressure is self-inflicted. It's time to lighten up.

I appreciate that our world, our culture, and our society has bred us to be serious. How many times have you heard "You need to take this seriously. Don't goof around; this is serious." That word, "serious," makes my entire body contract.

The only thing you need to take seriously is how serious I am about becoming not-so-serious. This one change will instantly take you to a state of happiness.

When you live in intensity, pressure, and seriousness, you are promoting chronic stress in your system. You are congesting your mind and creating overwhelm. You cannot access your creativity with ease, and you are far more likely to be triggered, angry, and frustrated on the regular. Seriousness keeps you stuck and unhappy.

Playfulness, on the other hand, is nonnegotiable when it comes to choosing happiness and LIVING your life.

How can you become more playful? What can you choose throughout your day to feel light and silly? You know, the things you did so easily as a child, before you started giving a shit what people thought of you and started believing you needed to be serious to be an adult. Ew.

THE WORK

Choose one of these things and do it now. I don't care if you're reading this on a train, if you're in a café, or if you're home alone. And if you're still worried about being silly, what's that about? (Now that you've learned so much, you can discover the thoughts and beliefs that are stopping you and change them.)

- Dance like no one is watching: shimmy, baby, shimmy.
- Sing the chorus of your favorite song.
- Go outside and sprint or skip up the road like you did when you were a kid.
- Tell your favorite joke, even if it is to yourself.
- Laugh out loud, an unadulterated, pure belly laugh.

I'm known to randomly do impressions of a monkey when I need to infuse a little levity. I do a killer monkey face and have a range of monkey sounds to go with it. It's genius.

Can you say that you are having enough fun and enjoyment in your life? This is something you need to infuse into every day. Here's the sentiment that I shared at my fortieth birthday bash, and it's something that I choose to remember every day: "It's time to lighten up, to take everything less seriously. It's only life after all, and no one's getting out alive, so calm the fuck down."

If that doesn't work for you, you can use my favorite levity-inducing mantra: "All of this is temporary." Again, "All of this is temporary." It feels good when you say it, doesn't it? The truth is all of this *IS* temporary. No matter what you are experiencing, feeling, or moving through, it's all temporary. Reminding yourself of this allows you to exhale, calm down, and relax. It allows you to not give your energy away, to not fixate on the perceived negatives. It influences you to feel lighter and happier instantly. You're welcome.

So, when you've finished racing around your neighborhood, telling jokes, and dancing like no one is watching, come back; I want to talk with you about gratitude.

Happy and Grateful

When we are consciously choosing happiness, a gratitude practice will maintain that choice and support our mental health and well-being along the way. Practicing gratitude is a requirement for your unbreakable happiness.

Gratitude is science. All of the research studies that have explored whether there's any value in practicing gratitude have resulted in one undeniable conclusion—practicing gratitude on the regular will improve your life. Period. I'm paraphrasing, but it works. Gratitude is scientifically proven magic.

When you practice gratitude, you are rewiring your brain to see the good in your life. The more you see, the more you experience. The more you experience, the happier you will feel. And the happier you feel, the more gratitude you will express. It's the perfect cycle, and it doesn't take long for it to become second nature.

I know that it feels easier to find the negative in any given situation. It's what humans are hardwired to find. There's nothing wrong with you if you have noticed that it's your default behavior. I promise, you're not broken. It's biological. Humans have a bias toward the negative. We can thank our long-lost ancestors for this because they needed this bias toward the negative. They had to become experts at finding the problem so that they could use that information to stay alive. It's thanks to that bias that the human race survived.

Hilda and Miriam heard a rustle as they reached for the juiciest red berries. They knew their men would be hungry after a hard day's hunting and as always, dinner would be on the cave floor ready for their homecoming.

"It's just the wind, Hilda, calm yourself," came Miriam's fateful last words. A saber-tooth tiger slashed her back, pushed her to the ground, and then dragged her deep into the forest.

"Shit, that's the last time I listen to Mrs. Positivity," Hilda thought as she sprinted back to her cave, leaving a trail of berries in her wake. "I knew that wasn't the wind."

If we had evolved with a bias to the positive, we wouldn't be here. It would mean death, the end of procreation, the end of the human race.

The problem we have now is that our brains are still wired for survival. Our brains don't know that our modern-day negativity isn't because our lives are in danger. Our modern-day negativity is a threat to our happiness, and we are now able to evolve in our own way through choosing a different thought and rewiring our mind.

Gratitude is one of the most effective ways to speed up that evolution. Think of gratitude as a muscle. As with any muscle, the more you train it, the stronger it gets and the more powerful it becomes.

Having said all of this, you also need to know that there are a couple ways that gratitude can be completely ineffective.

Gratitude is a meaningful practice. It is essential to FEEL the gratitude and to use your practice to cultivate a state that you experience.

If you use it to try and deny that you're experiencing sadness, for example, it can backfire. Imagine you are grieving the loss of a good friend. It's not okay to say, "Well, I should just be grateful for the time we had." You have to allow yourself to feel and respect what you're feeling before you choose another path. Then, of course, when you are ready, you can choose to feel grateful for the awesome person you had in your life.

Imagine you started your business full of enthusiasm and you launched a new program, but it bombed. Okay, yes, this is a personal example. I worked hard; I put together a badass program for entrepreneurs. I had the program plotted, the graphics were on point, and I was ready. I launched it, I did everything I believed I needed to do, and I waited for the entrepreneurs to sign up. Nothing. Crickets. No one wanted it. I sat, took a few deep breaths, and started to choose my response. Instead of slapping a ton of false gratitude on it, I chose to allow myself to feel into it, to reflect on what went well and what didn't. It was through that process that I was then able to have authentic deep appreciation and gratitude for myself and the lessons I learned. That is meaningful gratitude.

That leads me to the second way gratitude can be ineffective. If you're simply spewing what you're grateful for without connecting to the emotion of why you're grateful, it becomes a cold, obligatory checklist that provides no real value. It doesn't effectively rewire your mind and won't result in you feeling happier.

THE WORK

Here's the key to a meaningful gratitude practice that WORKS. Try it; explore how it makes you feel.

I feel grateful for _____ because _____
_____.

When you add the "because," you are inviting your mind to articulate why you are grateful, and that helps you connect to the emotion of it, which is the whole point.

Once you have written it down, read it over and over again. Read it until you feel it.

To really bring gratitude into your life, you need to practice it daily.

You can institute a morning or evening daily gratitude practice. Include this way of articulating gratitude when you journal, but also use "gratitude on demand" when you need a quick shift or change in perspective. Wherever you are and whatever you're doing, you can take a moment to think about something or someone you are grateful for.

Influencing Happiness

So many things influence our happiness, and we choose each and every one of them.

Think about the people in your life: the people you live with, the people you work with, the people you hang out with. Do they lift your energy levels or bring them down? Do they support and inspire you or suck you dry? What kind of conversations do these relationships fill your day with? Are you engaging in gossip and rumors, or are you discussing possibilities, ideas, and opportunities?

The company we choose to keep has a direct influence on how we feel. Some relationships in our lives can be toxic, and it's up to us to become aware of what those relationships are doing to us. This isn't about judgment of those people. Each person's journey is just as valid and valued as the next person's. This is about you and your ability to become aware of what is influencing your happiness.

These choices usually require some courage. You might be thinking about relationships you've been engaged in for years, yet you are now beginning to realize the impact these relationships have on you.

Janine was the Queen of Complaining, although by our second session together she had changed her title to "recovering complainer," which was a step in the right direction. We were discussing her friendships and I asked, "What do you and your friends talk about when you get on the phone?"

"Other people, always. We share news, have a bitch about idiots at work, and if anyone has annoyed us, we talk about that too."

"What would happen if you didn't do that, if you stopped complaining?" I asked.

She genuinely looked confused. "What would we talk about?"

"Yourselves, what you are working on, how you're feeling, what's going well for you, to name a few ideas," I suggested.

"Okay, I'll try it."

Not only did Janine choose to ask her friends different questions and talk about what was going well for her, she found that she wasn't complaining in other areas of her life. She was happier at work, talking with her partner about what was going well for both of them, and her energy levels increased exponentially. On top of that, her friends said that similar things were happening for them. Through making the choice to try a new approach to her conversations and set new boundaries, she had been a catalyst for change.

Complaining orients your brain toward the negative and keeps you in disempowering states. Each complaint is a directive to your mind, saying, "Let's be negative and feel like shit!"

While we're on this topic of cultivating more happiness, realize that if you are in a habit of complaining, you are choosing to block your flow of happiness. The people in your life influence and support certain habits and attitudes, so when you are creating change, taking a look at the people around you and the context of your relationships is essential. If you're surrounded by people who like to complain, think about how you can make a change.

THE WORK

You don't have to make any quick decisions on this. It's an opportunity to assess what's going on for you.

Think about the people in your life. As you were reading, someone may have come to mind. Grab your journal and write down, "How do I feel when I hang out with _____?" Then think about your thoughts before meeting up with them. How do you feel after you have seen them? How does your body respond when you think about them? How would you feel if they knocked on your door right now?

You might decide to fully disconnect from some people, and that's okay. Not all relationships are meant to be with you for life.

You might decide that with an agreement around boundaries, some relationships could significantly improve, and you might realize just how awesome some of the people in your life are and make a conscious choice to spend more time with them.

I recently attended a personal and professional growth event; it was a three-day immersive experience, super fantastic, but that's not the point. During a break, I ran to the bathroom and ended up in a twenty-minute transformational conversation with a lovely group of women. Yes, magic happens in the women's restroom. A young, powerful woman, getting ready to go after her entrepreneurial dream, was talking about how unsupportive her family was being.

She said, "I know they love me, but it doesn't feel like it right now. They keep trying to talk me out of it, and their comments are filling me with doubt. They are my family, and they have a huge influence on me. It's really impacting my dreams."

"The people who love you are coming from a place of protection," I explained. "They don't feel your conviction, they're not able to see your dream, and so they want to keep you safe. It is not because they don't believe in you or because they don't want you to be happy. It's because they cannot see your paradigm. This is their shit. You can decide not to be available for it."

Her eyes widened and she got it instantly. With that, she was able to see it differently and not let it in. She stepped straight back into her power, chose to have a conversation with her family about boundaries, and returned back to her state of happiness.

Choose the people you surround yourself with. Choose the people you want to exchange energy with. Your happiness and success depend on it.

The Power of Your Environment

Now onto one of my favorite happiness influencers—your environment. Yes, my hoarding friends, I'm talking to you. It's not just the people around us that we need to be aware of.

Your outside reflects your inside, and your inside reflects your outside.

If you have a collection of numbered birthday candles just in case eight years from now someone comes over to your house on their twelfth birthday and you will be prepared, this is for you.

If the clothes in your closet cover three size categories because you might, one day, be that size again, this is for you.

If you avoid the junk drawer in your kitchen because when you open it, you instantly feel overwhelmed, this is for you.

If you have kept the disgusting statue your mother-in-law gave you after an impromptu visit to an antique store, this is for you.

If you moved into your house, hated the color of the kitchen wall and still feel your heart sink when you see it, but haven't made the time to paint it, this is for you.

FUCK THAT. Your environment has a huge influence on your energy levels and is one of the most, if not *the* most, accessible thing to change. It's tangible. It's not like consciously, consistently rewiring and reprogramming your mind.

It takes choice and action. Boom, that's it.

You're worthy. You're enough. You can do what you want with your environment.

Organizing, purging, and redecorating are instant happiness inducers. You can create an environment that feels fabulous, and by spending time in that environment, it will influence the way you feel.

My sister, Barri, always gets a good laugh out of how much and how frequently I purge. She jokes and wonders how I still have clothes in my closet. I'm always going through my closet and giving stuff away. It feels good; it helps me feel at ease, and that is one of my desired, empowering states, so I make choices that align me to that.

Clutter makes me feel cluttered and overwhelmed, so I simplify and don't have bric-a-brac or small sentimental, decorative things everywhere.

You take this to the next level if you're ready to play BIG. How does the environment in which you live make you feel? If you hate the cold and it makes you feel low, move to somewhere sunny. If you cannot stand oppressive heat and humidity, move to the mountains. Sure, I'm simplifying, but you get my point. You're not a hostage of your environment. You can make choices that will change your life and support your happiness.

This is my one and only "environment rule," and I sincerely hope you make it yours too.

If it doesn't bring me a feeling of joy, it's out.

When I look around my house, if the furniture, the décor, the colors, or the setup itself doesn't induce a calm, instant feeling of yummy joy, it's out.

One of the most miraculous things I've ever noticed about the environment in which we live is the impact it has on our attitude and high-level feelings. Feeling sad? Go clean out your junk drawer. Feeling low? Go purge your closet. Feeling overwhelmed? Clean out your garage.

The Language of Happiness

Of all things that directly impact your happiness, by far the most significant is your language, those words which you think and choose to speak.

I have no doubt that you are grossly underestimating the power of every word that leaves your lips.

The words you choose are a reflection of your thoughts, just as much as your thoughts influence the words you choose. The words you choose bring you closer to how you want to feel. The words you choose create your experiences of your world. The words you choose orient your mind to positivity and empowerment or to negativity and disempowerment. The words you choose are directives to your brain, and the words you choose raise or lower your energy and vibration.

What makes you dread the annual visit to the doctor for your physical? What makes you totally uninterested in going grocery shopping? Your words. The way you speak about those things.

If you're about to visit the doctor and you're saying, "It takes forever, there is always a long wait, and I hate going," then guess what? You will dread the visit. You are responsible, and you are constantly creating your reality.

What if you chose these words instead? "I'm grateful I have a doctor to see. I'm going to bring the book I've been trying to find time to read and enjoy my downtime in the waiting room." How different does that feel? Still dreading the visit?

Your grocery store experience goes from "The lines are insane, the parking lot never has spots, and I don't feel like going" to "Yay! Food. I'm excited to go grab stuff that my family and I can eat together. It's so cool that I only have go down the road and get everything I need."

You can FEEL the difference, can't you?

As you continue to raise your consciousness, you will bring awareness to the words you choose. You will find that your feelings act as a guide to show you the power of the words you're using. The feelings you're experiencing are being directly influenced by the words you're choosing.

Let's dive into some language directives. These are key pieces of language that will support you in changing your life.

Stop using pervasive and permanent words like *always, never, every time, forever,* and *nothing.* They limit you tremendously. "I always take things personally." Instead, try using words like *sometimes, occasionally, not always.* It lightens that situation, and it lightens you. "Sometimes I take things personally."

EVERY WORD is a directive. So when you say *always* and *every time,* your mind is responding to that, following the instruction and saying, "Okay, got it! That's what we'll do; we'll always take things personally."

Your mind will always do what it thinks you want it to do. The way it knows what you want it to do is through your words because that's the way you communicate with it. Simple, right?

"I'm having challenges with my marriage, and it's going to be like this forever. Nothing ever changes." Your mind has been given a clear instruction. The truth about life is that all things are temporary. Using pervasive and permanent language just makes it harder for you to get unstuck, feel better, and change.

Stop using overly dramatic words that are, in truth, disproportionate to your reality. If you have a habit of catastrophizing, you'll use words such as "horrible," "terrible," "the worst," "horrendous," "appalling," "horrifying," "devastating." When you whip these words out, it's usually a dramatization. Yes, unfortunately we live in a world that does experience horrendous, terrible, devastating events, and that is when those words need to be used. However, in your daily existence, where you are choosing happiness, you've got to cut this shit out.

If you run late for a meeting, does it really translate into a terrible day? If you lose a client, was it really the worst? If you have an argument with your spouse, do you need to call your friend and say that things are horrible? If you're not at your fitness best, do you really look horrendous? Using these words will create your reality. Stop it.

Let me give you some juicy ideas about ways in which you can start making new choices around language. Yes, you know the first thing I'm going to say is that you need to become aware of your language and make choices as a result. You can easily upgrade your language choices:

- I have a ton of laundry to do; it never ends. Upgrade: I'm lucky to have clothes to fold.
- I'm so busy; I have too much going on. Upgrade: I have such a full life; I'm blessed.
- My kid is being such an asshole. Upgrade: One day her bold attitude will serve her well.

I've already talked about ditching the words can't and should from your vocabulary, but I'm just dropping this in here as a reminder while we're talking about the power of words. If you haven't already, ditch them, ditch them now!

So, are you ready to no longer chase happiness and finally choose to be happy right now?

Repeat our **Worthy Human Mantra** after me:

I am worthy. I am enough. I am powerful. I get to choose.

Choice #8
ARE YOU READY TO FALL IN LOVE WITH *Fear?*

"Everything you want is on the other side of fear."
— *JACK CANFIELD*

By now you've guessed what my favorite f-word is, but our journey together would not be complete without a real and raw conversation about my second favorite f-word. It is the single biggest block for every human, everywhere. It is fear.

Let's start at the very beginning; it's a very good place to start.

What Is Fear?

Fear, by definition, is an unpleasant emotion caused by the belief that someone or something is dangerous, likely to cause pain, or a threat to you.

There is so much in this definition that I love. Firstly, it's an "unpleasant emotion," and humans are pleasure-seeking beings. We aim to avoid pain and seek pleasure, so if fear is an unpleasant emotion, it's definitely something we won't want to feel. Secondly, it's "caused by belief," and with everything you've already learned about your inner power, you know that a belief is simply a thought you choose to think over and over and then it feels true. Beliefs can be changed.

Before we continue to dive deep into the topic of fear, which is one of my all-time favorite things to talk about, we need to draw a clear distinction between fear and danger.

Fear is designed to warn us when we're in danger, when you need to discern if a situation is life-threatening. You'll experience fear if you're swimming in the ocean and you see a shark's fin coming toward you. You'll experience fear if you start to cross the street and a car comes out of nowhere, heading in your direction. You'll experience fear if you're cooking and see flames appear from under the pan. These are dangerous situations, and in these situations, fear is helpful.

If fear only showed up when you were in danger, I wouldn't have this chapter to write, and everyone in the universe would be living their best life.

So, why does fear show up when you're not in danger?

Because fear is a physiological response that happens inside your brain every time you enter into the unknown or even think about entering into the unknown. Fear shows up when you want to try something new, when you want to make changes in your life, when you want to grow your business, when you want to speak on stage, when you want to have a crucial conversation, when you want to set a new boundary, or when you want to do something huge with your life.

Why? Because of science. Because of evolution.

Even though it's the twenty-first century and we can send messages through cyberspace, we can order something online and it's at the door in seven minutes, and we can video call a friend on the other side of the earth, the part of our brain that houses our fear response hasn't evolved at all. We are still operating with the same primal, reptilian part of our brain that we operated with during cavepeople days. You remember Hilda and Miriam, don't you?

So, when you were a caveperson (and yes, you were totally awesome then too with a great ass), the ONLY way to stay alive was to be on high alert for dangerous situations.

Your mind still has one principal function, and that is to keep you alive. That is all. It doesn't care if you are happy, fulfilled, killin' it in your business, having lots of great sex, enjoying time with your friends, prioritizing your well-being, making money, and feeling inner peace; its only concern is that you survive. The fear response is your mind's way of keeping you alive, and that response is triggered by stress and unfamiliar situations.

The irony is that for you to change your life from what you're experiencing now to your desired reality, you are going to come up against constant unfamiliar situations. Because to be different and to change, you inherently will have to enter the unknown, the uncertain . . . the unfamiliar. And to your mind, that means potential death.

Consciously, we know that is total bullshit. However, subconsciously our mind does not understand that. It means well, but the problem is that it's blocking you from EVERYTHING YOU EVER WANTED IN YOUR LIFE.

Fortunately for you, you get to change your relationship with fear. You are more powerful than the fear, especially once you fully understand it. Understanding is power.

Here's the best representation of fear that I can give you. You've seen *The Wizard of Oz*, right?

In the movie, Dorothy, the Lion, the Scarecrow, and the Tin Man were all traveling to the Emerald City to ask the Great and Powerful Oz for the things they needed. Dorothy needed to go home, the Lion needed his courage, the Scarecrow needed a brain, and the Tin Man needed a heart. That sounds simple enough, doesn't it?

On their way to the Emerald City, they were afraid because the Great and Powerful Oz was notoriously terrifying. No one had ever met the Great and Powerful Oz, but it was widely accepted that he had a loud, scary voice and he was in control of everything.

The group reached the Emerald City and made their requests to the Great and Powerful Oz. Just as Oz started responding, Toto, Dorothy's dog, jumped out of the basket he had been carried in and ran toward the curtains where the loud, scary voice was coming from. Toto pulled the curtain back with his teeth and revealed the (not so) Great and Powerful Oz. He was a tiny, four-foot-ten-inch old dude with a huge-ass microphone. He was the puniest, least scary thing ever.

The Great and Powerful Oz immediately pulled the curtain

closed and tried to continue with his loud, scary voice, but, of course, it didn't work. You can't unsee what you have seen.

Your fear is your very own version of the Great and Powerful Oz. It's an illusion.

What Are You Afraid Of?

Think about where you are in your life right now. Are you where you want to be?

- Is there a difficult conversation that you have been avoiding?
- Have you been thinking about that dream business but taken no action?
- Have you started a business but you haven't been promoting it?
- Do you daydream about going for a promotion but haven't actually applied?
- Have you avoided going to a party because you didn't know many people there?
- Has someone asked you to speak at their event but you declined?
- Have you been looking at the beautiful human at the gym but not asked them out?

All of these perceived problems are coated with fear.

I mentioned at the start of this book that I was once a part of corporate America. Well, I was the vice president of people and culture for a healthcare consulting firm, and yes, it was as exciting as it sounds. All was well, sort of; I kept saying that everything was fine. I couldn't find one tangible reason to make a change. Except, I wasn't "well" at all. I was going through the motions, checking the boxes, staying safe.

My gut was gnawing at me. In truth, it had been gnawing at me for a couple years: "You have so much more in you than you are giving. Is this really all there is? You cannot wake up day after day and do this. You were born for greatness. What are you waiting for?"

I had a gift for helping people and a deep desire to serve others in a meaningful, life-changing way. I had researched therapy, coaching, and other healing modalities. I had decided coaching was the winner, I had chosen the school I wanted to attend, and I did my due diligence and daydreamed about it for two years. TWO YEARS.

I stayed in the corporate job because I was scared. Every time I almost said yes to going back to school, I shrunk back into "It's fine" and carried on. I rationalized it: "I have a good job; I make good money. It's flexible. They like me, and I like them."

I was dying inside. I knew I had the capacity to follow my dreams, I knew I could do it, I could do anything. What I didn't realize at the time was fear's role in ensuring I didn't leave the job and go back to school.

Fear said, "Do you really think you can do this? What if it doesn't work? What if you invest in going back to school, and it amounts to nothing? What if you're not as good as you think you are? What if no one hires you? It's too much of a risk."

Then one magnificent night in January, I was sitting on a hotel balcony overlooking the ocean. I was quiet enough that I could hear myself: "Do it, Tracy. It's time. You are not going to get to the end of your life and look back with regret, asking yourself why you didn't take the chance. Do it, you were made for this." I got up from the chair, walked inside the hotel room, opened my laptop, and enrolled in the coaching school. Boom. Decision made. The fear was still there, but my power of choice was stronger. Through personal growth, learning, and experience, I have come to understand fear and its intentions. I have fallen in love with fear. Yes, fallen in love with it, and I have used its power for good ever since.

The Fear Rolodex

Here's what was really happening inside my mind and where the fear came from. It's exactly the same as what's going on in yours. Our fear response is biological; no one is exempt.

I was getting ready to play big, and that meant moving outside of my comfort zone, toward something unfamiliar. The first thing my mind did was look for evidence of a similar past experience. My mind was scanning to see if this potential move would be safe or unsafe. Remember, its singular purpose is to keep me alive.

Because I had no previous evidence of having done anything like this before, my mind couldn't find anything in its Rolodex, so it was labeled unsafe.

So the stress signals were released. *"Danger! Danger! Danger! The human might die!"* were sent to my amygdala, the part of the brain where my fear response lives and that activated a series of efforts to make sure I didn't take steps toward the perceived threat.

This shit makes so much sense, doesn't it? It will change your life.

The series of efforts included sending whispers of doubt, concern, and hesitation up into my mind. The perceived threat was kept at bay for those two years. But I was still daydreaming, still battling, and eventually, my connection to that which I desired won over the fear.

We're all grateful for that, aren't we? I'm here, showing up as my best self in the world and now you're holding my book in your hands. I didn't know this would happen. If I had known, I wouldn't have waited over two years.

Falling in Love with Fear

Fear still comes around, it always will. Just because I understand it and am madly in love with it, doesn't mean it has disappeared. On the contrary, we're now working together. This is precisely why fearlessness is not a thing. Fearlessness is a myth and quite frankly I believe the use of the word is a disservice to us all. Because if you believe in fearlessness, not only are you still feeling fear, but now you also feel like something's wrong with you because you're not fearless after all.

Fear is physiological, it is part of the human condition and it will arrive, on cue, every time you are about to embark upon something unfamiliar. Every time you think about or start to move outside your comfort zone and into uncertainty, like the most dependable dog you've ever known, fear will be right there, by your side.

There's nothing to be afraid of, fear is simply looking out for you.

Now that you understand what fear is and why it shows up, you can see it for what it is and love it.

In actual fact, when fear comes around, it's confirmation that you're changing. It's the clearest indication that you are expanding beyond your comfort zone and creating a life that you are madly in love with.

Fear means you're making shit happen!

When you choose to fall in love with fear, you are breaking your resistance to it. Remember that when you resist something, it persists, it gets louder and more powerful.

THE WORK

You have already experienced how powerful it is to take something from being across the table from you to sitting with you on the same side.

Now you're going to do the same thing with your fears.

You're on one side of the table, and fear is sitting on the other side. You can see what you're afraid of, it's right there, in front of you, in opposition to you.

Put your arms out, reach across the table and pick up your fear. Bring it toward you and sit it on your lap.

Talk to your fear. "Hey, I see you, I feel you, and I love you. I understand your intention is to keep me safe but I promise you I'm not in danger. I'm growing and this is going to be good for me. You can hang out with me if you'd like to, but only if I can use your energy to support me, OK? Let's do this."

Now you are in love with your fear. You have broken the resistance, because you brought it to you, you took Radical Personal Responsibility and chose to love it. Now you are fucking unstoppable.

Randi was a rock star client of mine. From the outside, everything looked seamless. She was in love with her girlfriend, living in the dream house, running the dream business, and really making shit happen. Everything she did seemed effortless, but all was not as it seemed.

"I really do have everything I have ever wanted, but I feel disconnected from it all. Why can't I enjoy the amazing life I have created?"

Even as Randi said those words, there wasn't any emotion attached to them. I knew that she was in love because she told me, and I knew that she had a successful business because she could detail what was happening in her working life, but I didn't feel anything as she spoke. She could have been reading her grocery list to me, not describing her life's work.

"What are you afraid of?" I asked.

Without emotion, she simply replied, "Nothing."

"If you were afraid of something, what would it be?"

At least she paused to think about this. I don't think either of us expected the conviction in her reply. "I would be afraid of showing that I'm vulnerable and frightened of losing everything because then, who would I be?"

Wow. "You're not used to showing a vulnerable side; I can see that. Vulnerability is unfamiliar to you, so it makes perfect sense that your fear response sees it as a threat. Your fear response is sending you messages day in, day out, telling you that any display of emotion or vulnerability might kill you. Of course you're feeling disconnected."

I took Randi through the exercise I have just shared with you. When she brought her fear of vulnerability to sit on her lap, she cried for the first time in years. We celebrated those tears and the fact that despite what her fear response had been warning her about, she didn't die.

Whether your fear response is triggered by something large or small, tangible or intangible, it doesn't matter. You still need to fall in love with the fear and work with it to create a new pathway in your brain so the unfamiliar becomes familiar. This isn't a one-off exercise. It's something you will need to do time and time again because I know that you have many changes ahead of you. Every time you do it, it's evidence that you are changing and progressing, so it's worth celebrating.

Fear Identification

We are faced with all kinds of fears. Some are easily identifiable, and some are camouflaged. Fear can be a sneaky little thing.

- Fear of failure
- Fear of the unknown
- Fear of confrontation
- Fear of success
- Fear of rejection
- Fear of not being enough, which is my least favorite because you are more than enough, always.

Because you have learned so much about the choices you have as a worthy human, the choices you have in raising your awareness and running your mind, you can powerfully move through all of these.

Let's take the fear of rejection and play with it because it's pervasive.

To start with, we need to realize that the fear of the thing, in this case rejection, is there because of the meaning we have associated with it. If you have made rejection mean that you are not enough, then you will fear it. In truth, rejection isn't even a thing. Being rejected has no tangible influence on your enough-ness.

If you fear rejection, you won't set boundaries. You will people please at the expense of yourself. You will not be unapologetically you. You will take things personally, and you will tolerate less than you deserve from others.

But you're choosing to believe that rejection is not a thing. So you don't have anything to fear.

You can bring your fear of rejection to sit on your lap and explain the situation. "Hey, little dude, thank you for trying to keep me safe. I appreciate it, but rejection isn't something I need to be frightened of, so together we're going to stand on that stage, talk about our work, and ask if anyone wants to come and hang out with us, okay?"

I had to put my theory into practice when I was confronted with an unsolicited opinion and my fear response saw a potential threat. I am constantly going live online; I love doing it, and I produce video after video. When you put yourself "out there," people have opinions. I have absolutely no control over that, nor do I want to have any control over that. What I do have control over is how I respond and the meaning I attach to what is happening.

So there I was doing a live video online, talking away, dropping knowledge, and having a blast. Viewers are commenting, and I'm coaching them through their questions. Then, this comment pops up: "You talk too much, your cursing is offensive, and you need to find God." WOAH.

This comment was available for everyone to see, and if I didn't have an amazing relationship with my fear response around rejection, it might have sabotaged me. In my world, rejection is not a thing. Rejection is a choice. I have faced this fear so many times that I have created a brand new pathway, and my amygdala doesn't even get alerted to the fact it's happening because it's not a threat. I simply said, "Cool, thanks for sharing" and kept going because you can't be rejected if you choose to believe it's not a thing and if you choose to not let it in.

This is the power of all of this work. You create who you are through consistency in the choices you make.

What about the sneakier, camouflage version of fear? I'm talking about fear's undercover agent—self-sabotage.

This is a collection of behaviors that interfere with your goals—procrastination, perfectionism, inaction, or numbing out with food, shopping, or drinking. Sound familiar?

These self-sabotaging behaviors are working undercover for one or more of the fears I mentioned earlier.

If you are interfering with your own ability to get what you want, you're afraid of something.

Belinda was a perfectionist. She had been planning to launch her business for months and had everything mapped out in meticulous detail; the planning folder really was a thing of beauty.

"How did the launch go?" I asked, sure that she had planned it for the week before our session.

"The website still isn't ready; I need to make sure the tone of the welcome page is just right, and it's not quite there yet."

"Haven't you had the draft ready for a while?" I asked, knowing full well that there were seven drafts in her planning folder.

"It was only really some draft outlines. It still needs work," she said, not convincing either of us.

"What would happen if you launched the website as it is?" I asked.

"I can't do that; what would people think if it's not just right?" She was visibly shaken by the thought of hitting "publish" and sending her imperfect (as defined by her) website into the world.

"I don't know; what would they think?"

"They would see that I'm not ready to do this, that I'm not good enough to be doing this."

"First of all, you are enough right now, all the time, and nothing you do perfectly or imperfectly impacts that. Period. Are you with me?"

"Yes, I know. I know."

"Second of all, what people think is none of your business. You can kill yourself trying to make something perfect, and you will never make everyone happy. You're not pizza."

Belinda laughed and started to loosen up. She was tracking with where I was going.

"So, if you choose to believe that you are enough and choose to not give a shit what people think, what choice would you make right now with your website?"

"Easy, I'd hit publish and be done with it. This feels so good."

And so she did. That was the day her relationship to her perfectionism started to change.

Perfectionism was working undercover for the fear of not being good enough. When she was working toward perfection, she was in control, and she believed she was enough.

The irony is that when I first met Belinda, she wore her perfectionism with pride. Now, she's freeing herself from the fear habit as she chooses to believe that she is enough and her website, or anything else, has no bearing on her enough-ness.

She continues to practice her new thoughts and beliefs and uses her tools of running her mind, the same tools and techniques you have now.

She brings awareness when her old habit of perfectionism is rearing its ugly head. She chooses to pause and breathe on purpose. Then she shifts into her new thoughts and beliefs of "I am enough, what people think is none of my business," and from that space is able to make new choices that align with how she wants to feel or the results she wants to experience. Belinda works the work, and it works.

If that's not awesome enough, every time she chooses something new, something that is outside of her comfort zone, e.g., embracing imperfection, she is giving her beautiful mind new evidence for her fear Rolodex, and it becomes easier and easier.

I know, it's so exciting. I love growth!

There was a lovely young lady who attended one of my events.

She stood up, stepped to the microphone, and said, "I have been in the personal growth world for a while now. I read the books, I attend talks like this, I gain some traction in feeling happier in my life, then it stops. I get excited about my new side hustle and start making more money, then I get distracted and stop taking action. Then I feel like shit about it and start all over again."

"What stops you?"

"I don't know. If I knew, I wouldn't stop."

"Fantastic, so let's keep going until you know. Shall we?"

"Yes, please."

"Great, so what will change in your life if you feel happy? What will change in your life if you do awesome with your side hustle and make lots of money?"

"I'll feel happy and I'll make money and my life will be awesome!"

"Yes, but if you really believed that, you wouldn't be sabotaging yourself and getting in your own way. Keep digging. Who will be impacted if you become happy and rich? What are you afraid of?"

The tears started to flow, which meant we were hitting gold!

"I'm afraid of what my family will think. I'm afraid of being more successful than them."

"Keep going; you're doing an amazing job for yourself."

"We didn't come from money. They usually are pretty judgmental about rich people and like to commiserate about it. If I'm happy and making money, I'm afraid it will disconnect me from my family. Oh my god. That's what stops me, holy shit."

Boom. There it was. The fear. The real fear, the real underbelly of her inaction, and procrastination sabotage.

This was one of those moments where awareness became curative.

She was able to see that this was a disempowering belief and it had to go so she could grow and experience the life she wants and most definitely deserves.

So, she worked the work by continuing to raise her awareness and to practice her new empowering thoughts and beliefs. And from that space, she continued to make new choices that aligned with her happy, money-making self.

Peeling back what lies beneath your self-sabotage feels like an awakening. A moment of revelation that, fortunately, you will never unsee.

Let's Get Visual

I love vision boards almost as much as I love fear. I was running my annual vision board workshop and sharing my enthusiasm for the process. You see, your mind communicates in images and words, so a vision board is crazy effective in supporting you to create your reality. In my vision board workshop, everyone gets crystal clear on what they want to achieve. We dig deep to identify and release why they don't already have those things and then create a board filled with the images of their life vision. It's a powerful process that really does work. It's so powerful because you are collaborating with your mind, using its rules. The mind receives communication about what you want through images and words and then works to get you what you want. If you're inputting that information in clear images and words every day, it makes sense that it works.

During the workshop, I lead the group through a visualization exercise. They're taken into a meditative state, and I guide them through my words and questions to a place of discovery. All in the name of getting clear on what they want, who they want to be, and how they want to feel.

THE WORK

You can take yourself through one of my favorite exercises; you might be familiar with it. Imagine that you're sitting in your rocking chair on your eighty-fifth birthday, sharing stories about the extraordinary life you have led. You have a captive audience, so make the most of it. Tell them about the adventures you have had, the fears you fell in love with, and the people you have met. Share the lessons you have learned, all the choices you have made, and tell them if you have any regrets. Really take the time to connect to all of this and write it down.

In the workshop, there were a couple of people who were struggling with clarity. They could share a fuzzy explanation of what they wanted, but it lacked detail. It's the detail that matters when you want to give your mind the correct information.

If you're someone who tried the exercise and couldn't get complete clarity about what you want to have achieved by the time you're sitting on your rocking chair at the ripe old age of eighty-five, I want you to answer this question: WHAT ARE YOU AFRAID OF?

Clarity means declaring where you want to be, which instantly pushes your thoughts into the unknown. That signals your fear response, and the warning flares cloud your mind, making everything foggy, leaving you with words like, "I don't know, I just don't know." Which is fine, if you want to be rocking in your chair telling people you didn't do anything with your life because you couldn't figure out what you wanted.

The other undercover agent at work could be warning your mind about something else: "If you have clarity, then you need to show up and take action. That sounds dangerous. We don't know what will happen if you do that." The fear response has been triggered as you're planning to venture into the unknown: "What if I fail? What if I succeed?"

Because when you're clear about what you want, it's time to take action. It's time to show up. When it's something you haven't done before and your mind can't find evidence of you surviving from it, it's marked as danger. Your mind will do everything in its power to stop you in an effort to keep you safe and alive.

THE WORK

I'm sure you are swirling with your own fears and how it may be showing up for you in your life. Take this time to check in with yourself.

- Which of these fears and fears in camouflage resonate with you?
- What fear do you have about growth or moving outside of your comfort zone?
- What are you **not** doing, where are you **not** taking action because of fear?
- What will it cost you to **not** become aware of, then choose to fall in love with, your fear?
- Knowing yourself and being completely honest, how does your fear show up (procrastination, not taking action, hiding)?

Dear Fear

If you're ready to completely change your relationship with fear, I'd like to invite you to join me in one of my favorite exercises—the Dear Fear letter. I don't know anyone who calls their fear John, but it's a similar idea to the well-known "Dear John" letter.

It's something that came to me on a run one afternoon. I was making some pretty big decisions, and fear was popping up everywhere. I was inspired to write fear a letter, a Dear John, we-need-to-break-up-or-change-our-relationship, kind of letter.

I came in from my run, opened my laptop, and magic came out. I felt totally liberated. This is it, my unedited Dear Fear letter.

Dear Fear,

It's not you. It's me. No, really, it's me.

We've had an interesting run, and ultimately, it's not going to work. Our dynamic sucks. It's time for me to take personal responsibility and take my power back.

I have let you lead and control this relationship, and it's not healthy for me. It's holding me back from my potential in life. Not to mention, it's not fair to you. I don't want to be mean and hate you and wish you weren't around. It's such a waste of energy!

And yes, I know what you're thinking… you're just trying to protect me. You want what you think is best for me. You just want me to be safe. And I appreciate that, truly. The thing is, I want a hell of a lot more than that.

I want deep happiness, I want to grow, I want to thrive, I want to create a business and legacy that impacts thousands, then millions. I want to speak on big stages, I want to be a best-selling author. I want to say no and not feel like shit about it. I want to put myself out there and not worry about what people will think. I want to say yes and figure it out later. I want to make time to slow down and enjoy the moment, to nurture my soul and well-being. I want to embrace and seek discomfort because I know the next levels of my awesomeness and fulfillment lay on the other side. And that's just the beginning...

And I know that you are simply doing what comes naturally. And I also know that you will always be around because you're a part of me and we have been together for our entire lives.

So, I'm redefining the terms of our relationship (and no, it's not negotiable, and I'm not interested in your opinion ... you've led long enough, and we've seen where that's gotten us).

When you show up, I will acknowledge you and appreciate you, but I'm running the show. I will always know you have good intentions but truly no fucking idea what I want or what matters to me.

I will allow you to hang out and come along with me, but from now on, we will sit on the same side of the table, and you will help me by using your energy to add confidence and conviction to what I want. If you try to inflict any opposing thoughts, you won't be allowed to hang out at all. Are we clear? Good.

I know that every time I think about or do something unfamiliar or uncomfortable, it's your tendency to make me afraid because you want me to stop. The thing is, I'm not in danger. I promise. It seems like danger to you because you think everything's going to kill me, but it's not danger, it's just new and uncomfortable.

And sure, if I'm ever in actual danger, like walking down a dark alley or if I'm near a hot stove, you can take the lead. Otherwise, trust me. I am super powerful, and I know where I want to be and where I'm trying to go.

You need to accept and embrace that I am seeking the unknown and the unfamiliar. It's the only way to create the life and business of my dreams! So, please get used to it because it is not changing anytime soon and the bottom line is, I am more powerful than you. And I'm not being mean, I'm simply letting you know the new lay of the land, the way our relationship is going to go from now on, because I refuse to tolerate anything less.

I also want to say thank you. Thank you for always looking out for me. For protecting me. For showing up at every possible tiny moment or situation where I wasn't completely comfortable. I always wondered why you never showed up to relax on the couch with me... I know now it's because I was safe and comfy, and you don't like to show your love for me unless you feel like something's wrong.

So please know this, NOTHING'S WRONG. In fact, everything is right. So super, exciting, awesomely right.

XOXO

Powerful, Limitless ME

So now I give this gift to you.

THE WORK

Write your Dear Fear letter. You can use the answers to the questions you asked yourself earlier. Take a look at how fear has prevented you from living your best life up until now. Then make a choice about how you want your relationship to be from now on.

The only requirement is that it starts with "Dear Fear, It's Not You, It's Me."

And yes, I totally want to read them. Post them online, tag me, and make sure you include #ilovefear so I can find them.

A Leap of Faith

I'm choosing not to end our journey together without talking about the relationship between fear and faith.

Faith is a powerful force that is always available to you and that will bring you calm and ease when you're facing fear. It means that we have complete trust or confidence in someone or something far bigger than you and me.

Read that again: COMPLETE TRUST or CONFIDENCE in SOMEONE or SOMETHING.

To me, faith is fully and unconditionally believing in something greater and bigger than myself, and when it comes to releasing myself from fear, from feeling afraid, faith is a powerful antidote.

It's about trusting that you have come from something greater, that you are connected to something greater, and that something greater is cocreating with you and always has your back.

It doesn't matter what you call "it": God, Universe, Source, whatever works for you. The important, nonnegotiable thing is the knowing and acknowledgment of its truth. You are not alone, you are not doing this alone, you are not expected to do this alone, it was never intended that you would do this alone.

Let me be really clear: I am not talking about faith in any religious context whatsoever. Faith in this context is not connected to any religious beliefs or associations unless that is what serves you and that is what you choose.

I was born and raised Jewish, and culturally, I associate with that. When it comes to what I put my faith in, however, it's all-encompassing. I choose to put my faith in the infinite wisdom of the universe and everything she has to offer.

Why am I sharing this with you as our journey together is coming to an end? Well, partly because I believe that it's part of the deal when you're raising your awareness and choosing your path. But also, it's because it's healing, it's empowering, it's calming, it's uplifting, and it's got your back. You're going to need that, in the face of fear, when you step up and take Radical Personal Responsibility.

With the insane power you possess, which is more awesome than anything you can imagine, it's important to know that you're not alone. This "source" is with you and within you, all the time, whenever you need it.

Have faith and trust in the "source" that connects us all, that creates miracles, that reminds us of our connection to one another and the true oneness that comes with being worthy humans.

The "source" offers you strength, courage, confidence, and support when you are in moments of darkness, of human experience. You can take a deep breath, surrender, and have faith that you are exactly where you need to be.

When you are about to take a big leap, make a new choice, step into the unknown, and leap with faith, she will give you the energy and confidence you need.

When you are asking, "What the actual fuck?" because life is doing that thing that life does, you must pause, take a deep breath, and believe that everything is happening for your highest good because it is, even when you are unable to see what it is in that moment. You will see it soon, I promise.

Fear and faith have something in common. They both ask us to believe in something we cannot see.

I see you, and I believe in you. You've got this.

Repeat our **Worthy Human Mantra** after me:

I am worthy. I am enough. I am powerful. I get to choose.

~

So, there you have it, my beautiful, worthy friend.

The keys, the blueprint, the roadmap to grow; expand and show up for this magnificent gift we call life.

Although this is the end of the book, it's only the beginning of the journey.

I invite you to use this book as your guide, your personal growth bible. Go back through and work the work. Practice the how-tos and all the exercises throughout.

It's amazing and necessary to feel inspired, but change comes from what you choose to do with that inspiration.

The work works when you work it. All you need to do is choose.

You deserve to heal. You deserve the life of your dreams. You deserve to let go of what's held you back. You deserve to spend the hours of your days feeling how you want to feel.

You deserve to be the happiest person you know.

What happens from today forward is based on your power to choose. All of it.

And now you have a deep understanding of just how many choices you have.

You no longer ever have to wonder why you are where you are or why you're not feeling how you want to feel. You no longer ever need to look outside of yourself because you now know and understand that you have everything you need inside you to experience and create your best life.

You have all the power. You always have, and you always will.

Now and forever, BE the solution.

You have from this very moment until however long you're here, may that be until you're over one hundred years old, to choose. To consciously create the life you want.

Choose who you want to be, how you want to feel, what you want to create in this world, how you want to act, what you want to hold onto and what you want to let go, how much of your energy you want to waste, and how many fucks you want to give.

I will leave you with this, as it is the quote that made me cry and lit a fire under me simultaneously. It underpins everything I choose in my life and how I show up for my work in this world:

> "Someone once told me the definition of hell:
> on your last day on earth, the person you became
> will meet the person you could have become."
> **— ANONYMOUS**

Yeah, I know. It hits hard, and that's the point. The person you get to become is completely up to you.

You are limitless. You are powerful. You are enough. You are a worthy human.

Treat yourself well.

Tracy

About the Author

Tracy Litt is a Certified Mindset Coach, Rapid Transformational Therapist, speaker, and author. As Founder of The Litt Factor and Worthy Human, her passion for personal growth shines through in the transformation of her clients and the empowerment of her merchandise line. Through Tracy's constructive, direct, and loving insight, countless individuals have transformed their lives from the inside out. Tracy's ultimate mission is to support individuals in cultivating a phenomenal relationship with themselves, thus igniting their limitless potential. Tracy lives in Lake Worth, Florida, with her husband, David, three teenage daughters—Taylor, Maddy, and Zoe—and their dog, Sunny. Learn more about her work at TheLittFactor.com.

CPSIA information can be obtained
at www.ICGtesting.com
Printed in the USA
BVHW030216231219
567560BV00001B/15/P